TALES FROM THE
NEW ENGLAND PATRIOTS
SIDELINE

TALES FROM THE
NEW ENGLAND PATRIOTS
SIDELINE

A COLLECTION OF THE GREATEST
PATRIOTS STORIES EVER TOLD

MIKE FELGER
WITH ERNIE PALLADINO

FOREWORD BY STEVE GROGAN
EPILOGUE BY BILL BELICHICK

SPORTS
PUBLISHING

Sports Publishing books may be purchased in bulk at special discounts for sales promotion, corporate gifts, fund-raising, or educational purposes. Special editions can also be created to specifications. For details, contact the Special Sales Department, Sports Publishing, 307 West 36th Street, 11th Floor, New York, NY 10018 or sportspubbooks@skyhorsepublishing.com.

Sports Publishing® is a registered trademark of Skyhorse Publishing, Inc.®, a Delaware corporation.

Visit our website at www.sportspubbooks.com.

10 9 8 7 6 5 4 3 2

Library of Congress Cataloging-in-Publication Data is available on file.

Cover design by Tom Lau
Cover photo credit: AP Images

ISBN: 978-1-68358-121-5
Ebook ISBN: 978-1-68358-125-3

Printed in the United States of America

CONTENTS

FOREWORD

Sixteen years. That's how long I played football for the New England Patriots. I look at it this way: The average career of a professional football player lasts four seasons, and that means I played with four generations of Patriots. Hall of Famers like John Hannah and Mike Haynes. Great players like Stanley Morgan, Steve Nelson, Russ Francis and Pete Brock. Close friends like John Smith and Don Hasselbeck. I could go on, but no one would have the time to hear all the names.

I know the Patriots organization has taken its lumps over the years, but I always felt playing here was a great experience.

When I arrived for my first training camp in 1975, I rented a house from tight end Bob Adams, who had just been traded. It turns out Bob left behind a book on the Patriots, so I picked it up and read it. That's when I learned about some of the team's history. Crazy stuff. I found out about the fire during a game at Boston College. I found out about a guy named Bob Gladieux getting called out of the stands because the coach needed an extra player, and Gladieux making the tackle on the opening kickoff. I found out that the players were once told not to turn down their bed sheets because the team didn't want to pay extra for their hotel rooms. And on and on.

Some of the stuff was pretty ridiculous, but I didn't care. I was just happy someone had drafted me. I had a neck injury in college, and some doctors had questioned whether I should even be playing. I was also worried about making the roster. Jim Plunkett, a Heisman Trophy winner, was the quarterback and I knew coach Chuck Fairbanks wasn't about to sit him down. So when I got on the field that camp I just tried to show them I was an athlete. I played running back for the scout team. I kicked when John Smith was having some leg problems. I did anything I could to make the team.

I did, and when Plunkett got hurt during the season, I was the one Fairbanks turned to. I didn't know what that meant for the future, although Jim seemed to. Jim was a very quiet guy, as was I, and we didn't speak much that first year. But I remember coming home on the airplane after the last game in '75. He walked by me and said, "Good luck, kid. I hope you have better luck here than I did." He obviously knew he wasn't going to be around the next season.

Suddenly, I was the starting quarterback—and for the next 15 years I fought to keep the job. I fought through good seasons and bad ones. I fought through challenges from young players and high draft picks. Sometimes I lost the job and had to fight to get it back. Sometimes injuries caught up to me.

The injuries. It's what people seem to remember most about my career. I had a lot of bumps and bruises along the way, but I played through most of them. The only time I probably shouldn't have been out there was in San Francisco in 1980. We had Matt Cavanaugh coming off knee surgery, and I had two knees bothering me to the point where I couldn't bend them. They asked me to play the game because they didn't want to take the chance with Matt. So I wound up playing and throwing five interceptions. I got crucified in the newspapers, but no one knew I was playing on two bad knees.

That was the time I hurt the most physically. It's probably the time I hurt the most emotionally, too.

Then Tony Eason got here and perceptions seemed to change. All anyone could talk about was my toughness. I remember telling Tony one time that the worst thing they did to him was keep me around after they made him the starter. Everyone just compared him to me, and it wasn't fair. He was probably as good as me or better, but he didn't have that toughness—and everyone let him know it.

Like most of the guys I played with, I considered the 1976 team the best I'd ever been on. That was the Patriots team that should have won the Super Bowl. The playoff game in Oakland—we got robbed. But with the players we had, we thought we would be playing for championships for a long time. Then a lot of things started happening and it just didn't get done.

We were popular at times, but nothing like it is now. That's probably the biggest difference. Today, the Pats are equal to the Red Sox. For most of my career, we weren't even close. We were actually the fourth team in town, behind the Celtics and Bruins, too.

I thought the first time we climbed the totem pole, the first time football got the attention it deserved around here, was in 1985 when we went to the Super Bowl. I remember driving to the airport to go play Miami in the AFC championship game and seeing people stop their cars on I-95 as we drove by. Waving and honking all the way to the airport. It was a great feeling.

We filled up the stadium for a few years after that, and then it seemed to go in the other direction. I finally had to retire after the 1990 season, which was really a dreadful year. Bill Parcells came a few years later, and it's been top of the rung ever since.

As a former player, it's been fun to watch what's gone on the last few years under Robert Kraft and Bill Belichick. It's amazing to see the facility they have now. I just recently saw the locker rooms at Gillette Stadium for the first time, and I admit I took an extra second in the showers. They were huge. At Foxboro Stadium, the hot water ran out after a few minutes.

I'll be honest. The first emotion I had when they won the Super Bowl in 2001 was envy. Jealousy. I saw them running around the field and the confetti falling down, and all I could think about was that we were that close. Still, after they beat St. Louis, it was the first time I felt good about putting on a Patriots hat since I retired. It was nice letting people know that I was one of the people who laid the groundwork for that—in a previous life, of course.

The recent success has led more and more people to look back at the previous life of the entire team. And they should—it's a rich history. I get a lot of dads who come into my sporting goods store, grab their kids, and point them in my direction: "Do you know who this guy is? Do you know what he did?" And the kids have no idea. I'm just the old guy working in the store.

One day, I waited on a lady for about 20 minutes trying to find exactly what she needed. After I went behind the counter to write up the order, she turned to me and said, "Does Steve Grogan really own this place?" And I said, "Yes, ma'am, he does." Then she asked, "Does he actually come into the store?" And I said, "Yes, ma'am, he's here every day."

She recognized the name, but she had no idea it was me. I finally had to tell her. I get that a lot.

For some reason, I don't think Tom Brady has the same problem.

—Steve Grogan
Mansfield, Massachusetts
July, 2006

INTRODUCTION

The spring of 2004 felt like a pinnacle for the New England Patriots. They were fresh off their second Super Bowl championship and were less than a year away from claiming their third in four years. It was a time when the team, once considered one of the most woebegone franchises in all of American sports, established itself as a dynasty, a generational organization to rival those of the Packers in the 60s, the Steelers in the 70s and the 49ers of the 80s. The first edition of this book was written that offseason, and in the introduction we made the obvious statement that the Pats had gone from being a laughingstock to being an elite, that after years of floundering they had emerged with one of the best coaches, quarterbacks and owners in the league.

It's now over a dozen years later and it turns out that statement wasn't quite right. It turns out we undersold it. That was far from their pinnacle.

It's turns out the Pats have arguably the best coach, quarterback and team in the history of football. They are no longer "one of" the best. They stand alone. It turns out Bill Belichick and Tom Brady aren't just the singular figures of their time. They are the greatest of all-time.

In other words, the gap between what the Patriots were (1959-1999) and what they are (2000-present) has grown even larger—as impossible as that seemed back in 2004.

The last 13 years have been, to use a word, eventful. Mostly good eventful, but really just eventful.

So what's happened since this book was first published?

Other than, in no particular order, three more championships, five more Super Bowl appearances, a perfect season, two all-time, heart-stopping Super Bowl wins (Seattle and Atlanta), one all-time, crushing Super Bowl defeat (Giants I), a season-ending knee injury to Brady, after which the team still won 11 games, 12 more division titles, six straight (and counting) appearances in the AFC title game, two cheating scandals—one of which was so fiercely contested that it nearly ended up in the Supreme Court—two lost first round picks, a four-game Brady suspension, after which the Pats still won a title, an alleged murdering spree by a star tight end (Aaron Hernandez), 162 regular season wins (an absurd average of over 12 per season) and 19 more postseason victories? Other than that? Not much.

The stories in this book detail what happened before things got good. And while those years produced no more than a sliver of the team's current success—the stories are just as rich. And as I sat down to write this new introduction and reacquaint myself with the history, I was struck by the parallels and the contrasts.

For example, in going over the Patriots' 1976 playoff loss in Oakland (the roughing the passer game), it struck me how the Pats' misfortune that day seems to have completely flipped on their opponents in the Belichick era. Read about that game and all the things that had to go against the Pats for them to lose it, and you'll feel what a fan of the Seattle Seahawks felt like after Super Bowl XLIX, or a fan of the Atlanta Falcons felt after Super LI. The Pats now win those games, in roughly the same fashion. When it matters most, everything goes right for them, and nothing goes right for the opponent.

And if you had told someone in 1976 that 40 years later one of those two teams would have five Vince Lombardi Trophies on the shelves of their state of the art new stadium and would be a jewel franchise of the league, and that the other would be unable to survive in their decrepit old building and end up in Las Vegas after over 30 years without a championship, well, let's just say that most people back then would have admitted the "Vegas Patriots" had a certain ring to it. Instead, it's the Raiders headed to the desert, their "Commitment to Excellence" era paling in comparison to what the Patriots have achieved.

Speaking of stadiums, where the Patriots play is something that a modern Pats fan hardly even considers any more. Gillette Stadium may not be the most expensive or elaborate building in the league, but compared to where the Pats called home over their first four decades, it stands as the eighth wonder of the world. Stadium issues hung over the franchise for decades, overshadowing most everything that happened on the field or sideline. From Fenway Park (one of the least suitable dual-purpose stadiums in America) to all three major local colleges, the Patriots were everywhere over their first 12 years. Then they finally got their own stadium in 1971—and it somehow got worse. This book will give you the lowlights of the Pats' time at Fenway, Boston University, Boston College, Harvard and Schaefer/Sullivan/Foxboro Stadium. We'd have included some highlights but there really weren't any.

But no matter where the team played, turmoil followed. We may think of the modern Patriots as having their share of controversy (Spygate, Deflategate, numerous contract battles, etc.), but it's nothing compared to the tension, dissension and dysfunction that permeated through whatever halls the Pats happened to call home at the time. We all were watching, for example, when ESPN's Tom Jackson, speaking of Belichick, told us in 2003 that the Patriots "hate their coach", and we thought it couldn't get much worse than that. Wrong. That was child's play compared to the way Patriots players of the early 80s felt about Ron Meyer (1982-84).

"A fraud," said guard John Hannah. "I chased him around the stadium one time trying to kill him."

You could write a book on the coaching issues alone. Where to start? Clive Rush electrocuted himself at an introductory press conference in 1969, had a nervous breakdown and drank himself out of the league. Chuck Fairbanks was one of the few early Patriots coaches who knew what he was doing, only the internal strife led him to pursue a new job (at the University of Colorado) while he was still on the clock in New England. That led to the absurdity of the season finale in 1978, when Fairbanks was kicked out of the Pats locker room before the game at the Orange Bowl on Monday Night Football. With the country watching, the Patriots then rolled out not one, but two, replacements, "co-head coaches" Ron Erhardt and Hank Bullough. They lost by 20 points. Somehow, Fairbanks was allowed to come back to coach the first home playoff game in Patriots history, which they promptly lost by 17 points. Then there was good guy Dick MacPherson, whose positivity was thought to be unbreakable, until the Pats broke it. He had to take a leave of absence due to a stomach condition brought on by stress in his second season.

As for ownership, there can be no bigger contrast than the one that exists between Robert Kraft and his predecessors.

Yes, the Krafts can be tough at contract time, but if you think they are tight with the finances, you should read up on Billy Sullivan.

"Like pulling teeth from a hen," said Larry Eisenhauer, a former star defensive end. Eisenhauer once had to hold out for a $500 raise.

The stakes were much higher in 1977 when star linemen Leon Gray and Hannah had agreements worked out with coach Fairbanks, only to have the Sullivans veto the deals. The subsequent holdouts of Gray and Hannah derailed the '77 season and led to the departure of Fairbanks the following year. Ask players from that era what prevented that talented team from winning a championship and most will point to the Sullivan family ownership.

Yes, the Kraft tenure has been at times tumultuous. It's hard to imagine now given the patriarchal status Kraft enjoys, but there was actually a time when he was referred to as a "fat assed millionaire" by state house speaker Tom Finneran. There was a time his coach, Bill Parcells, told a local newspaper that "I didn't want any more to do with this guy." Everything with the Patriots is now kept in-house, which was hardly the case early in Kraft's ownership. It's startling to go back and read how open the festering wound was between Parcells and Kraft at the Super Bowl in New Orleans.

Kraft redeemed himself with the hiring of Belichick, which son Jonathan Kraft has since called one of the greatest trades in the history of sports. Hyperbole? Maybe not. A first-round pick for one of the greatest football coaches ever? Jonathan Kraft may have a point. Remember, hiring Belichick was no slam dunk given his negative ratings coming out of Cleveland.

Either way, the decision to hire him by Robert Kraft stands in stark contrast to the decision Billy Sullivan made in 1969, when he had a choice between Colts defensive coordinator Chuck Noll or Jets offensive coordinator Rush and chose the latter after allegedly changing his mind when Rush's Jets upset Noll's Colts in Super Bowl III. Noll, of course, won four Super Bowls and is in the Hall of Fame. Rush won five games in two years before mercifully being shown the door.

Speaking of Jonathan Kraft, he's developed a reputation in some quarters for being a bit combustible. But, again, modern fans have no idea what it used to be like. Check out the picture of Pat Sullivan being challenged to a fight by Howie Long during a playoff game in 1985. Or ask Hannah Chuck Sullivan's role in reneging on the Grey and Hannah deals in 1977.

"Oh Daddy! You can't do this!" Hannah recalled Chuck telling his father, Billy. "You're going to bankrupt the team. Please, Daddy!"

That's how the team used to be run. Now? We'll just answer that with the bottom line: In 2016, Forbes magazine valued the Pats, which Kraft bought for $172 million in 1994, at $3.4 billion.

Yes, financial management certainly has changed in Foxboro. There was once a time when the team's ownership felt it was a good idea to get into bed with the Jackson family and their advisors, Don King and Al Sharpton, for a concert tour. Pat Sullivan still can't bring himself to admit how much money was actually lost on the venture. Whatever it was, it forced out the Sullivans. And then, as tended to happen to the Pats in those days, it actually got worse. Again.

Subsequent owner Victor Kiam was so inept in his brief ownership tenure that he was once shut out of his own owner's box during a game because of a dispute (with Kraft). That was actually a cute story compared to his comportment during the Lisa Olson incident. Just a complete bozo. Unlike Kraft, he never understood the value of the stadium lease and was soon gone.

As for the quarterback position, a fan born after 1995 has no conception of what it was like around here. Excluding injury and suspension, it's been Tom Brady under center for 17 straight years. Seventeen years where there has been no question who the No. 1 quarterback is. Seventeen years of excellence and stability at the most important spot in pro sports.

Compare that to other 17-year stretches in team history. If you followed the Patriots between, say, 1978 and 1995, you saw the Pats employ 14 starting quarterbacks. Fourteen. That 17-year stretch was bookended by Steve Grogan and Drew Bledsoe—two pretty good players. Now hold your nose for what came between them: Matt Cavanaugh, Tom Owen, Tony Eason, Tom Ramsey, Bob Bleier, Doug Flutie, Marc Wilson, Tom Hodson, Hugh Millen, Scott Zolak (sorry, Zo), Jeff Carlson and Scott Secules.

It's a different world now, from the quarterback on out. This book aims to remind you of just how different.

I'll take the time here to thank the people who helped me with this project, most notably those who consented to interviews.

Pat Sullivan was tremendous. It's easy to look down on his family's tenure, but the truth is that, for the most part, they were good people with the right intentions. And they never had the benefit of Tom Brady falling into their laps with the 199th pick of the draft.

Raymond Berry was as humble and gracious as we all remember him. Hannah was as bitter. Pete Carroll was passionate in his defense of his time here. John Smith and Randy Vataha were great. Thanks also to Gino Cappelletti, Steve Nelson, Andrew Tippett and Lisa Olson. When I spoke to Darryl Stingley (rest his soul; he passed away in 2007) his voice was weak but his memory was sharp. Others who helped me and have since passed include Bill Lenkaitis (2016), Bucko Kilroy (2007) and Fairbanks (2013).

I'm thankful to Grogan for the foreword and, especially, Belichick for the epilogue. I still remember the hand-written pages he sent me from Nantucket early that summer in 2004. There were a couple of revisions, and his first draft had a few paragraphs on yet another subject that deserves its own book—his history with Parcells and the circumstances that finally brought him to New England as head coach. He ultimately decided not to go with it. It's a chapter that's been covered elsewhere over the years and will no doubt be addressed again when the definitive Belichick tome is written. In the meantime, this book is lucky to possess a true rarity, at least as of 2017: a written, first-person narrative by Bill Belichick. Again, we thank him for it.

Finally, I'm thankful to my family—Sara, Emma, and Tessa; Rocky, Georgia and Dan—for their support and love.

This book begins Nov. 16, 1959, the day Billy Sullivan was awarded the team. It ends on Jan. 27, 2000, the day Belichick was formally hired. In between is the story of the New England Patriots before they became one of the great dynasties in all of sports. The first 40 years weren't nearly as successful, though they were nearly as entertaining (not always in a good way, obviously).

The first edition of this book was published just months after the Pats met with President George Bush in the Rose Garden of the White House to celebrate their second Super Bowl title. This edition is being published just months after the Pats met with Donald Trump to celebrate their fifth. In between, they also met with Barack Obama to commemorate their fourth. Has any team, in any sport, ever been so successful for so long that they met with three sitting presidents over 15 years? Probably not.

There was a time when the only way the Patriots would get to see the White House was on a tour bus. Now they get there so often that they're starting to run into old friends. It turns out Trump nearly purchased the Patriots during that hyper-tumultuous time after the Sullivans were forced to give up ownership in the 80s. Instead, Robert Kraft got the team and he and Trump became lifelong friends. Over the years, Trump also grew close with Brady and Belichick. That has led some to dub the Pats "Team Trump," which may or may not be a good thing depending on which way you lean. But we can all agree it's a major step up from what they were for over 40 years of their existence: Team Turmoil.

—Michael Felger
Boston
April 2017

1

THE AFL

Humble beginnings?

That cliché doesn't begin to describe how the Boston Patriots came into the world in 1959.

That was the year former Notre Dame coach Frank Leahy was helping the fledgling American Football League put together its enterprise. The league had secured seven franchises and was looking for an eighth, so Leahy called his old friend Billy Sullivan in Boston and asked if he would be interested in bringing a team to Massachusetts.

Sullivan was—even though he had no money, no place to play, and no real fan support. Two previous pro football teams, the Boston Yanks and the Boston Redskins, had failed in the Hub. Sullivan had also failed in his attempt to lure the NFL Chicago Cardinals out east a few years before.

But what the heck? What did Sullivan have to lose?

Sullivan emptied his savings account—he liked to brag the balance was only $8,300—and took out a loan to reach the $25,000 franchise fee. Then he brought in nine other investors and sold non-voting public stock to raise working capital. Finally, Boston University allowed Sullivan to use its rusty old stadium for games.

The name "Patriots" was chosen after a fan vote. The "Pat Patriot" logo was actually a newspaper cartoon drawn by Phil Bissell of the *Boston Globe*. Sullivan liked it so much he adopted it for his team.

Bingo, presto. Pro football was back in Boston.

Kind of.

BED SHEETS

The Patriots in that era were "professional" in name only.

They held their practices at East Boston High School, where the team worked out on a field near Logan Airport. Travelers driving in and out of the airport today can still see the field, jammed as it is between highway ramps and rental car lots. Most people who notice it usually say the same thing: "What an odd place for that!"

Team meetings were held in a dank room beneath the stands. Unfortunately for the players, the budget didn't allow for chairs or projection screens. Instead, game films were projected onto bed sheets and players sat on milk crates.

"The sheets were hung from water pipes near the ceiling," said Patriots hall of fame member Gino Cappelletti, who played every game in the 10-year history of the AFL. "They'd tape them up there. Then they'd set the camera up on a box. And for some reason they used to deliver a lot of milk over there. So we found the crates and sat on them. The offense sat facing one way and the defense sat facing the other, watching film at the same time. So you had coaches making comments back and forth. Sometimes it got a little confusing."

Conditions on the road were just as tight. A famous example occurred in 1961 when the team traveled to Buffalo for an August preseason game. The flight arrived early in the day, so the team arranged for a midday stopover at a local hotel. The rooms cost $10 apiece, only there was a catch. If the bed sheets were messed up, the hotel would charge $15 per room. So the order went out: If any players decided to take a nap, they had to sleep above the covers. Some obeyed, some didn't.

"We were told if removed the covers we'd be fined our per diem, which was $10," said Larry Eisenhauer, a defensive end from 1961-1969. "I just told my teammates, 'For ten bucks I'm going to get under the covers.' And I did."

The typical salary for players was around $7,500 for the season. Eisenhauer said he made $9,000 his first year and then asked for a raise to $10,000 after making the AFL all-rookie team. Eisenhauer

Larry Eisenhauer once had to hold out over $500. *(New England Patriots)*

had already received a $500 bonus for the award. Billy Sullivan agreed to Eisenhauer's request, but when Eisenhauer saw the final wording on the contract, he noticed a net gain of only $500. When he asked Sullivan about it, the owner said he included Eisenhauer's bonus from the year before.

"I ended up holding out of training camp for $500," said Eisenhauer. "It was like pulling teeth from a hen."

Despite those problems, there was a sense of common purpose in those early days, and most players were forgiving. After all, where else were they going to go? Most of them had failed in their attempts to make an NFL roster, and they needed the AFL to survive if they wanted to be paid to play football.

"There was only one thing that mattered. That we got our paychecks after the game," said Cappelletti. "Because as you talked to guys around the league, you found out some guys weren't. We never missed a single payroll. And whether Billy Sullivan was having difficultly or not, no one really knew or cared. All teams were in the same boat. You could go around to each team and they'd probably have a similar story. You talk about adversity, but at the time we didn't know it. It was very important for all those players in the early years for the league to succeed. There was tremendous pride among us for the league. It's what defined us."

Patrick Sullivan, the youngest son of Billy Sullivan and a future GM of the team, pointed out that the entire AFL was run on a shoestring.

"It's not like we had an exclusive on a Spartan existence in that league," said Sullivan. "The fact that we had high school-type locker rooms, well, everyone in the AFL had the same situation. You should have seen Buffalo. They had these stairs into the clubhouse, but they were built for baseball players in the early 1900s. So all the guys had to take off their pads to squeeze in. That was the league, not just us."

Cappelletti was one of the players who was asked to sleep above the covers that day in Buffalo, and he didn't think twice about it.

"It was brutally hot that day, so [coach] Mike Holovak said if you want to go up and sit in air-conditioned rooms and watch TV and be comfortable, go ahead. Just don't get under the covers," said Cappelletti. "It was a very simple and understandable request. The media made it out to be like it was this cheap thing. But we didn't care. Who wanted to get under the covers anyway?"

FRIDAY NIGHT LIGHTS

As hard as it would be to believe today, the Patriots in the early 1960s actually had to compete with a team from New York for the allegiance of New England sports fans. That's right; when the AFL started in 1960, Boston was Giants Country—as in the New York Football Giants. After all, the established NFL franchise was the closest geographical pro football team to Boston, and Giants games were broadcast into the region every Sunday. For years, it was all fans in New England had.

Then along came the Patriots.

But the upstart team from the upstart league wasn't about to butt heads with the New Yorkers. So the decision was made to play home game on Friday nights, far removed from the Sunday afternoon tradition of Giants football.

"We knew we had to go a long way to win over the fans around here," said Cappelletti. "In that first year or two you'd tell people you were with the Patriots and they'd say, 'Who are they?' It was just something we had to overcome. But that decision to play on Friday nights worked out quite well for us, because we had the lead game and then had the weekend off, which wasn't a bad deal."

By the mid-'60s the AFL had received a lucrative new TV deal with NBC, and the Pats found themselves playing more games on Sunday at 4 p.m.

"And this was just when football was starting to really take off and people were really hungry for more," said Cappelletti. "So we started coming on at 4 and people started watching—just because of their hunger for football. Then we started to build these names—Lenny Dawson, Lance Alworth, Earl Faison. They all became figures of professional football. And this is how we got to diminish the images and the roles of the Giants players who were well known around here. That is how it all started for us."

FRUIT COCKTAIL

What was covering the Patriots like as a media member in the early days? There is no one more qualified to offer a glimpse than Ron Hobson, the longtime reporter for the Quincy, Massachussetts, *Patriot Ledger* who started covering the team in its inaugural season in 1960. Hobson became the *Ledger*'s lead beat writer in 1961, and his first day on the job gave him a taste of the craziness he would be writing about for the next 40 years.

"They had this regular press luncheon every Tuesday at the Kenmore Hotel," said Hobson. "So I showed up that first day and, naturally, I was late and not quite sure where I was going. I was lost, actually. So I wandered downstairs and turned a corner down a hallway and there was Billy Sullivan on one end and [head coach] Lou Saban on the other. And they were having this big fight. They were screaming at each other. I said, 'Holy mackerel. What's that all about?'

"So I ducked my head and found my way upstairs to have my fruit cocktail and a nice meal. But right then Billy came into the hall and told everyone, 'I've fired the coach!' He then said [assistant] Mike Holovak was going to be the new guy."

Hobson got right up and drove over to BU field, where he and a small group of reporters found Holovak collecting jock straps in the equipment room.

"He had no idea what had happened," said Hobson. "I was the one who told him. Holovak found out he was the new coach from me.

"And I never got to eat my fruit cocktail."

WATER BALLET

People seem to forget that the Patriots actually provided a respectable on-field product through much of the 1960s. Unfortunately, that success always seemed to be eclipsed by some off-field issue. It was a condition the Pats would suffer under for the next four decades.

The Pats had the honor of hosting the first regular-season game in AFL history against Denver on September 9, 1960. The only problem was that Broncos coach Frank Filchock was able to walk into BU stadium the day before and watch the Pats run through their plays during practice. Final score: Denver 13, Patriots 10.

The Pats wound up with a losing record that first year (5-9), but from 1961-66 they posted five winning seasons and compiled a 47-31-8 record. The team's first quarterback was Ed (Butch) Songin, a 36-year-old probation officer. Songin had been a star at Boston College but had been out of football for six years when the Pats came calling. He threw 36 touchdown passes over the team's first two seasons.

Songin eventually gave way to Babe Parilli, who was a part of the Pats' early Italian flair, which included teammates Nick Buoniconti, Tony Sardisco, Tony Romeo, and Cappelletti. Parilli was voted to the three AFL All-Star teams and was the Pats' first star. He still holds the Patriots record for touchdown passes in a season with 31 in 1964.

Other early stars included defensive end Bob Dee, who scored the first touchdown in AFL history when he fell on a fumble in a preseason game at Buffalo, defensive tackle Jim Lee "Earthquake" Hunt and running back Ron Burton, the first ever Patriot draft choice.

In 1963, the Patriots advanced all the way to the AFL championship game in San Diego against the Chargers. But, true to form, the best tale from that appearance came off the field.

The Pats stayed at the Stardust Hotel in San Diego, which was a favorite for its golf course and big outdoor swimming pool. The Stardust also had a second pool that was used for water ballet shows, which people watched from an adjacent bar with huge glass windows looking into the bottom of the pool. The week of the game, Eisenhauer was enjoying a swim with his father when inspiration struck him. Eisenhauer suggested that he and his father try the second pool, which he said was heated and for the team only. His father agreed.

"Naturally, all the players were at the bar drinking, waiting for the girls in the little bikinis to get in the water and do their thing," said Eisenhauer. "The next thing you know, Bam!, my father is in the pool, swimming around, not realizing that everyone can see him. He was totally enjoying himself. I jumped in. Then some of the players got up from the bar and joined us. The story later came out that we were naked. We weren't, but we still put on quite a show."

Picture the stunned look of the tourists who had come to watch a water ballet show, only to see Eisenhauer, his father and a dozen intoxicated football players frolicking in the water. It was synchronized swimming—Patriots style.

The police were called. Eisenhauer's father was questioned and released. That Sunday, the Pats lost to the Chargers, 51-10, giving up 610 yards of offense.

GINO

When Cappelletti showed up in Boston in 1960 from the Minnesota prairie, his resume was typical of many AFL players. In other words, he was an unknown, overlooked player of indeterminate age who had been passed over by the NFL. Today, Cappelletti stands as one of the living legends of the AFL, someone who writers continue to push for induction into the Pro Football Hall of Fame in Canton, Ohio.

Cappelletti starred at the University of Minnesota but was considered too small and too slow to make it at the next level. After college, the best he could do was land a job in a semi-pro league in Canada. Cappelletti soon returned to Minnesota to tend bar and play in the local flag football circuit. His only shot at the NFL came in 1959, when he had a quick, and unsuccessful, tryout with the Detroit Lions.

When the AFL started the next year, Cappelletti called the Pats and was invited for a tryout. When the team asked him how old he was, Cappelletti gave an answer that was less than 100 percent truthful.

"We won't get into that," said Cappelletti. "You can say I was a 25-year-old rookie. But I wasn't alone on the age thing, believe me. That's what the league was comprised of, guys that had been rejects or just couldn't make it. Guys who were wrestlers, guys who worked in

Gino Cappelletti played in every Patriot AFL game. *(New England Patriots)*

factories or bars. There were so many like me. I think everyone fudged on their age when they came in."

Like most of his teammates, Cappelletti continued to hold down a second job through most of his playing career, working as a teller at nearby Suffolk Downs race track.

Cappelletti played a full decade for the Pats and never missed a game. He started out as a defensive back but ultimately settled in as a receiver and place kicker. He remains the team's all-time leading scorer with 1,130 points. (Adam Vinatieri is in second, finishing the 2003 season with 944 points). Cappelletti led the AFL in scoring five times and was a five-time All-Star. By anyone's measure, those are Hall of Fame numbers.

Cappelletti has been with the Patriots organization through everything, serving as a radio broadcaster from 1972-78 and 1988-present while taking three years (1979-81) to serve as the Pats' special teams coach. If there were such a thing as "Mr. Patriot," it would be Cappelletti.

What does he remember most from his 36 years of service to the Pats?

"I don't really point to any one thing, just the sense of pride we all shared representing Boston and the AFL," he said. "That was our determination, to make this team and this league go and have the city of Boston be proud of it. We saw what was happening with the Celtics and the Red Sox, and we saw how the town embraced those teams. We knew we had to get in line.

"I'm an AFL guy, so the thing that means the most to me is when the Jets beat Baltimore in the Super Bowl. And then when Kansas City beat Minnesota the next year. That made everyone ever connected with that league feel so proud. And that's what that league was all about. It didn't matter that it was a competitor. It was a team representing our league. And all the things we put up with and all the things that we fought for came to fruition in that game."

Meanwhile, the Hall of Fame veterans committee is asked to take up Cappelletti's case every summer. One of these years, they'll probably get it right.

THE MAN IN THE TRENCH COAT

The Patriots' first home field also happened to be the former home of the Boston Braves National League baseball team. Boston University had taken over the stadium, but Billy Sullivan still knew it like the back of his hand from his days as the Braves' public relations director.

That didn't make it any more comfortable for the players.

"They built us a locker room up on top of a second floor of a maintenance shack," said Cappelletti. "We'd have to walk up 16-20 steps with cleats on to get back up and down. We had one shower, a circular thing, and you could fit maybe six people under it at one time. That was it for the facilities."

Crowd control at the stadium wasn't exactly sophisticated, either, and the Pats' first ever home sellout (25,063) on November 3, 1961, against the Dallas Texans proved to be a memorable night.

On the final play of the game, with the Texans going for a tying score, a fan slipped out of the crowd surrounding the end zone and ran in front of Texans receiver Chris Burford as a pass was headed in his direction. The ball fell incomplete, and before anyone could tell what happened, the fan disappeared back into the crowd. He was never heard from again, and the Pats had a 28-21 victory.

According to legend, the mysterious fan wore a trench coat and a top hat similar to the one favored by Sullivan. Some people, only half-jokingly, claimed it was the Pats owner who had come out of the crowd to save the game for his team.

Cappelletti's version?

"First of all, he wasn't in a trench coat," he said. "It was just a normal windbreaker. But what happened was that on the play before, with just a few seconds left, Burford caught a long pass and the officials ruled him down at the 1-yard line. So all the people ran out of the stands and onto the field to celebrate, thinking the game was over. But the officials said there was still one second left. So they had to push all the fans back off the field, and they couldn't get them all into the stands. They ended up being seven or eight deep around that end zone.

"On the next play, [quarterback] Cotton Davidson went back and looked for Burford again. Then that guy ran out, waved his arms in front of Burford and the ball sailed over his head. ...We saw it on film the next day and laughed like hell. It was beautiful. No one really saw what happened at the time. It was too confusing."

Was it possible that the mysterious man was Billy Sullivan?

"I think it was some bookmaker from East Boston trying to protect a bet," said Cappelletti.

A DIFFERENT LEVEL OF DISCOMFORT

If the majority of Patriots players were accepting of their meager conditions in Boston, then what happened when the team traveled to New Orleans in 1961 for a week of practice and an exhibition game against the Houston Oilers constituted something else entirely.

Because of the segregation laws of the deep south at the time, the Pats' African American players were forced to lodge separately from their teammates, who stayed at a "whites-only" hotel.

Other teams had run into similar situations and had dealt with them differently. Vince Lombardi's Green Bay Packers, for instance, refused to enter any establishment where the full team wasn't welcome. The fact that the Patriots couldn't do the same thing makes this one of the most disappointing tales in team history.

"It wasn't in Boston where I had the big letdown in terms of where we played or practiced," said Houston Antwine, a star defensive tackle for the Pats from 1961-71. "It was in New Orleans when the ball club split up. That was a big letdown to me. Nobody really outlined the situation to us until the last day of camp before we headed down there. We didn't know until then. The coaches tried to be apologetic, but that's the way it was going to be."

The Pats practiced together as a team during the week, and at the end of the day the black players went one way and the white players went another. So much for "team."

"It just didn't feel right," said Antwine, who is African American. "I don't know why it happened, but it did. And it was a lousy, disastrous game we had that weekend [a 20-10 loss]. I had really considered the team like a family. We did things together. We won ballgames, we lost ballgames—all together. We laughed together. And now all of a sudden there was a wedge in there. That was a downer, it really was.

"But we overcame that."

FENWAY PARK

Even in 1963, Fenway Park was a woefully outdated facility for professional sports. Today it's a relic. But when the Patriots moved into the longtime home of the Red Sox after three years at BU, it seemed like they had reached the big time.

"It was such hallowed ground, it was a thrill to play there," said Eisenhauer. "It was a recognition for the league and the team. We were

The AFL Patriots played some games in Fenway Park. *(New England Patriots)*

able to say we played where the Red Sox played. It was recognition that we were able to command that type of venue. We loved it."

The field was laid out from the third-base line to the bullpens in right field. The best seats in the house were from the temporary bleachers that were constructed in front of the Green Monster in left field. And because the seats along the first-base line were so low to the ground, both teams set up their benches on the far sidelines so fans in the box seats could see. Players said they would routinely take advantage of the arrangement by edging up to the dividing line between the teams and listening to the opposing play calls going onto the field.

Gil Santos called the games on radio from a rickety, temporary booth that sat atop the grandstand roof. On windy days, Santos feared the small shack would be blown off into the stands below. There were no facilities on the roof, so Santos had to climb a ladder to and from his perch if he needed to go to the bathroom.

But Fenway was still Fenway, which meant it had an ambiance and character despite the conditions. Just as the old park can be a great place to watch a baseball game, it also provided a special atmosphere for Patriots football. After games, fans would come on the field and mingle with players.

The Patriots' stay at Fenway came to an end in 1968, a year after the Red Sox' "Impossible Dream" World Series appearance. The Sox, perhaps a little too confident in their success, figured that if playoff baseball was in their future, they didn't want the Pats sharing the field until after the scheduled end of the World Series. It turned out to be wishful thinking, as the Sox didn't play another postseason game until 1975.

Anyway, the Pats left with mostly fond memories of their time on Yawkey Way.

"My favorite Fenway Story came from Jack Kemp," said Pat Sullivan, referring to the former Buffalo quarterback, U.S. congressman, and presidential candidate. "He told me the reason he got into politics was because of what someone said to him on the field after a game. He said a Pats season-ticket holder came up to him and told him he was a good-looking guy, that he reminded him of President Kennedy and that he should really consider going into politics. So he did. But Jack later told me that the fan never forgave him, because he ended up registering as a Republican.

"When I asked Jack why, he just shook his head and said, 'Because the fan was Tip O'Neill.'"

2

THE
"BS" PATRIOTS

Patriots history is littered with strange people and bizarre events. But there may have been no greater concentration of both than the period from 1969-72.

It was a time when ineptitude raged on the sidelines, in the front office and on the field. Sometimes it was so bad it was comical. Mostly it was just sad. The Patriots covered the spectrum. There were electrocutions and fires, back-room deals and nervous breakdowns. There were drunks on the field and drunks coming out of the stands to make tackles.

"Obviously, we weren't very successful," said linebacker Marty Schottenheimer, who somehow recovered from his two seasons with the Pats (1969-70) to later become a successful NFL head coach. "One year we played at Boston College, and another year we were at Harvard. One year we went 2-12. But that was a totally different era. There were a lot of distractions."

That four-year span saw the team get a new name, a new stadium and a new Heisman Trophy-winning quarterback. None of it was enough to cover up the madness that raged through the organization.

SHOCKING

The New York Jets' stunning upset of the Baltimore Colts in Super Bowl III changed the face of the NFL. Unfortunately, it also changed the face of Patriots football.

With the Pats suffering consecutive losing seasons under Mike Holovak in 1967 and 1968, Billy Sullivan decided he needed to make a splash with his next head coach. And what better way to do that than to narrow his list of candidates to the assistants whose teams were playing for the championship? Sullivan was said to prefer Colts defensive coordinator Chuck Noll, but he also liked Jets offensive coordinator Clive Rush. Sullivan had to wait until after the Super Bowl before making a final decision, but the assumption was that Noll would be headed to Boston after the Colts beat up on the upstart Jets.

Of course, Joe Namath and the Jets had other ideas. And Sullivan, figuring he'd get hammered by the local media if he chose the losing coach, abandoned Noll and settled on Rush.

History turned at that moment. Noll went on to win four Super Bowls in Pittsburgh and is in the Hall of Fame. Rush went on to become a laughingstock in New England.

Rush's second appearance in front of the Boston media, a press conference to introduce general manager George Sauer, proved to be a fitting harbinger. Getting things started, Rush walked to the podium and stood in front of the group of assembled reporters. Then he put his hands on the microphone.

"All of a sudden he started screaming at the top of his lungs," said writer Ron Hobson. "And his hair started going out in all directions. His jaw locked. It took everyone a few seconds to realize he'd just electrocuted himself."

Rush was saved by Dan Marr, one of Billy Sullivan's board members, who realized the microphone wasn't grounded and ran to the outlet to unplug it. Rush collapsed to the ground and lay there for several minutes before regaining his feet.

"He finally gathered himself and got up," said Hobson. "Then he returned to the mike and said, 'I heard the Boston media was tough—but this is ridiculous.'

"It was the only funny thing he ever said," added Hobson. "I think that shock ended up lasting a long time."

THE BLACK POWER DEFENSE

Whether it was the electrocution or something else, Rush proved almost immediately that he didn't have the temperament or nerves to be a professional football coach. Gino Cappelletti remembers the chain-smoking Rush calling him into his office after his first team speech and asking the kicker, over and over, if he had done a good job.

"It was like he was in a panic," said Cappelletti.

Actually, there may have been a good reason why Rush was so unsure of himself that day.

"We had one of those laughing bags, and we were passing it around during his speech," said Larry Eisenhauer. "He'd be in the middle of saying something, and all of a sudden he'd hear this laughing. He'd stop and look around and try to figure out what was going on. And we'd just pass the thing from guy to guy. It was beautiful."

Rush was a nervous man who drank to calm himself. He was erratic and inconsistent. Players remember loud nights in hotel rooms and disorganized practices. During one game in San Diego in 1968, Rush lost his composure to the point where he was penalized twice for unsportsmanlike conduct, and Billy Sullivan had to leave his box and join him on the sidelines.

"He was wild. He was crazy," said defensive end Houston Antwine. "He'd hit that booze, man. I remember he called me into his office before practice one day. I was a captain and a team rep now, and I'm sitting there with my pads on and he opens up this cabinet behind his desk and it's filled with Jack Daniels! He pulls out a bottle and starts tugging on it. I'm just trying to get out to practice. I'm like, 'Uh, Coach?'"

Added radio broadcaster Gil Santos: "When you talked to him, if you asked him a question, he'd answer it at 500 miles-per-hour and say a lot of things that weren't really relevant to what you just asked him. But he'd say it in rapid-fire succession and he'd say the same thing over and over again. You'd walk away from the conversation saying, 'What the hell did he just say?' It was really strange."

The tip of the iceberg was Rush's "Black Power" defense. Trying to capitalize on the civil rights movement of the time, Rush came up with the idea to start a defense made up entirely of black players. The only problem was the Pats didn't have enough African Americans to fill out all the positions, so Rush converted some offensive players to defense just so he could fulfill his scheme.

"Our director of player personnel at that time was Rommie Loudd, who was a black guy," said Pat Sullivan. "And I can remember Loudd sitting next to my father in the press box one day and saying, 'I think this guy has completely lost his marbles.' Even the black guys thought it was nuts. And that was an era when everyone had afros, so it was really the weirdest damn thing to see out on the field. The players thought it was nuts. Everyone thought it was nuts."

"Nuts?" said Schottenheimer. "That's an understatement."

According to Antwine, the scheme was merely an attempt by Rush to motivate the team.

"He was just looking for something to inspire us," he said. "I thought it was a nice little gimmick myself. It was kind of inspirational. I think Clive was a little bit 'out there' anyway."

The best thing you could say about Rush's tenure was that it ended quickly. In 1969, the Pats lost their first seven games and finished 4-10. In 1970, the Pats started 1-6, Rush had a nervous breakdown and was fired in early November. The next day, Rush showed up to a Patriots' press conference with his tiny pet dog. He approached Hobson, asked him to hold the leash and then attacked local television reporter Clarke Booth.

"Clive at that point was definitely having some issues," said Pat Sullivan.

FIRE!

The Patriots' nomadic existence reached its zenith in 1969 and 1970. With Fenway no longer an option and BU also out of the picture, the Pats played their home games at the two remaining local colleges that would take them—Boston College and Harvard. The Pats lasted just a year at each location, suffering through more problems on and off the field.

The Pats' first exhibition game in 1970, against the Redskins at BC's Alumni Stadium, was a sign of things to come. With the game in full swing, a faint smell of something burning began to fill the air. Soon the smell became stronger, and suddenly reporters in the press box were shocked to see fans running out of the stands and onto the field.

The bleachers were on fire. Apparently, someone (not Clive Rush, thankfully) had dropped a cigarette into a rubber hole for the pole vault underneath the stands, and everything went up in flames.

"I remember sitting on the bench and all of a sudden there was this commotion in the stands behind us," said Eisenhauer. "The next thing

In the Patriots' one season at Boston College, an exhibition game was delayed due to a fire in the stands. *(New England Patriots)*

you know, the refs blew the whistle and the fans started running out past us. We all sat there on the field for a while, just talking to the fans and watching the fire. The fire department showed up and put it out. No big deal."

The game resumed and the Pats were thumped 45-21.

HARPO

It has been said that the Patriots often resembled a Marx Brothers movie.

They even borrowed some of the cast members.

According to legend, an unheralded reserve running back by the name of Bob Gladieux went to the 1970 season opener at Harvard Stadium against the Dolphins as a fan, even though he had been cut by Rush just a few days before. As the story goes, Gladieux imbibed heavily before the game and then staggered into the stadium with a friend to watch the pregame warm ups. When the teams headed back into the locker rooms to prepare for the game, Gladieux's friend got up for a round of beer, which is just when the public address announcer sent out a call for Gladieux to report to the Pats' locker room. When Gladieux did, he found that Rush had just cut defensive back John Charles after he refused to sign a contract in the trainer's room. That left an open roster spot, which Gladieux agreed to fill. He was assigned Charles's spot on the kickoff team.

Back up in the stands, Gladieux's friend returned to his seat with his tray full of beer and hot dogs when he noticed Gladieux was missing. He sat and waited. Puzzled, he turned to another fan and asked if he had seen Gladieux. Just then, the Pats kicked off and the question was answered when the PA crackled with the words, "Tackle, Gladieux!" When the friend looked to the field, he was stunned to see Gladieux running to the sidelines in full uniform.

Fact or fiction?

"You bet it's true," said Gladieux, who went by the nickname "Harpo" because of his wild mane of curly blond hair. "And it becomes a bigger feat every year that goes by."

Gladieux said Rush had actually cut him just days before the 1969 opener as well, only the coach never told him to his face. Gladieux found out on the nightly news. Then, in 1970, virtually the same thing happened, as Gladieux found out he was among the last cuts in the newspaper. This time, Gladieux responded by going on a bender.

"I started on Thursday," said Gladieux. "And I was all over the place for the next three days. On Sunday I woke up on Beacon Hill someplace, and, hey, I was a sentimental guy—so I decided to go see the game. I called my friend. He had a six-pack of Schlitz and I had a nice bottle of port. We had a nice time with it. After we got to our seats, I turned to him and said, 'Okay, Jack, first round is on you.'

"He left and that's when the PA called my name. Sure, I was a little confused. I looked up at the sky and thought God was talking to me. But I made my way down there, and when they told me to put on a uniform I thought, no way. I'm in no condition to play this game."

"He was hammered," said Pat Sullivan. "I mean, completely."

"But just then a light went off in my head," added Gladieux, "and it had a dollar sign on it. Of course, they put me on the kickoff team, and I said to myself, 'Okay, Harpo, just stay away from contact, you shouldn't be doing this.' So when I saw the wedge coming at me, I tried to dodge it by running around it. But wouldn't you know it? The guy ran the wrong way and crashed right into me....We beat the Dolphins that day."

It's true. The 27-14 final was Rush's last win as a head coach.

Meanwhile, Gladieux stuck with the Pats for a few more years. He eventually settled back in South Bend, Indiana, where today he owns a travel agency with his wife. Talk about a long, strange trip.

UPTON

Today, Upton Bell is known in Boston as an off-beat television and radio personality, the guy with the weird hair, wild socks and outrageous opinions. Only those of a certain age remember him as the Patriots' general manager. And history will show that his short, two-year (1971-72) tenure was as tumultuous a period as the team has ever known.

And that's saying something.

Bell came to the Pats as a whiz kid with credentials and bloodlines. He was the son of legendary NFL commissioner and team owner Bert Bell, and as a personnel executive in Baltimore, the younger Bell had helped build the Colts into a Super Bowl champion. Bell was 32 years old when Colts owner Carroll Rosenbloom convinced Sullivan to hire him as GM.

Bell arrived in New England to find turmoil. Billy Sullivan was in the midst of an endless power struggle with his board of directors, and no one knew who was in charge. There was back-biting and shifting allegiances. No one trusted anyone. And, of course, there was no money.

Bell knew he was in trouble when he stepped to the microphone for his introductory press conference. Only mildly aware of what had happened to Clive Rush two years before, Bell was greeted with the following catcall from a wise guy in the crowd: "Don't touch the mike!"

"It was Dante's Inferno," said Bell. "I came here to fix a football problem, which I thought I could do. But I found out in the end that it was the least of my problems."

Bell and Sullivan clashed from the start, and the relationship never improved.

"It got to the point where I had a phone installed in my house that was an exclusive Billy Sullivan line," said Bell. "If it rang, I knew to not answer it."

It turns out Bell was a fitting figure in Pats' history—colorful and overmatched. His marquee personnel move, trading for Dallas running back Duane Thomas, was ultimately reversed when Thomas showed up to training camp with a raging drug problem. He refused to get down in a three-point stance and was sent back to Dallas. Bell claimed then-president Richard Nixon had talked him into the deal while the two sat next to each other at a Hall of Fame dinner in Canton, Ohio. Bell's one draft, in 1972, produced 15 players who were quickly forgotten. In two seasons, Bell's Patriots went 9-19.

It's probably no coincidence that Bell never worked again in the NFL after leaving the Patriots. He later got involved with the Charlotte franchise in the short-lived WFL and then settled in behind a microphone.

Bell blames Sullivan for his failure to land another NFL job.

"There was a real problem with Billy Sullivan and myself," said Bell. "I wouldn't call it black-listing, but the owners were so powerful in those days that if enough things were said about you, you might not work again."

Pat Sullivan is well aware of Bell's lament.

"I've heard Uppy's version of history," said Sullivan. "I like Uppy. He's a character and everything else. We get along. But he's very bitter about my dad, because he fired him. And I wish he'd get over it. I keep on saying to him, 'Uppy, you've got to move on. For Christ sakes, how old are you now? You're a lot older than I am and you're still yakking about all this stuff?' I mean, you never hear me say anything bad about Victor Kiam [the Pats owner who fired Sullivan as GM in 1991]. You move on.'

"But I'll tell you what Uppy was just like," added Sullivan. "He was just like George Sauer. And he was just like Clive Rush. And just like [future team CEO] Sam Jankovich. And just like [future VP of football operations] Patrick Forte. He was like those guys because he came highly recommended from another owner. Sauer and Rush were highly recommended by [Jets owner] Sonny Werblin. And San Jankovich and Patrick Forte were highly recommended by [Philly owner] Norman Braman to Victor Kiam.

"And the fact is that, in the NFL, if you have a competent executive, you don't want to recommend them to anybody. You only recommend somebody with the hope that it will screw them up. Uppy had been with the Colts for years. And the fact that Carroll Rosenbloom, who was absolutely one of the smartest, shrewdest, and most devious guys in the history of the game, would say, 'Hey, Billy, I've got this guy,' that should tell you something.

"And my father bought it hook, line, and sinker."

THE DEAL

Soon after arriving in New England, Bell developed a singular obsession: He wanted to fire coach John Mazur.

The only problem was that Billy Sullivan refused to let him do it, and the Pats won just enough in 1971 to make the decision a borderline call. Late in the season, Sullivan added to the controversy when he appeared on a local television show and claimed Bell did not have the power to hire or fire the coach—it would have to be a decision by the board of directors.

Bell fumed, and with the Pats owing a 5-8 record heading into the season finale at Baltimore, the young general manager was granted the opportunity to plead his case in front of the full board. The meeting was supposed to be top secret.

Bell showed up to find reporters and television cameras everywhere.

"I wanted to fire Mazur, I didn't care if we had won 10 games," said Bell. "And all along Billy Sullivan was seething. Because of a lot of our success, he was no longer getting the credit or the blame, and I don't think he liked it. People were writing things like 'Brilliant young GM,' and I think it really pissed him off.

"So I stood up in front of the board and told them my understanding, that I had the authority to make this decision. I liked John Mazur personally, but I thought he wasn't the guy for the job. We had to bite the bullet despite the success we were having. I said if we didn't do this, we would live to regret it."

So Bell and the board made a deal:

If the Pats lost to the Colts by more than a touchdown in that final game, Mazur was out. If the margin was less than seven points, or the Pats somehow won, Mazur got to stay.

"I knew that Colts team," said Bell. "I helped build it. They had won the Super Bowl the year before and were playing for home-field advantage in the playoffs that game. I figured we'd get blown out."

But in true Patriots fashion, just the opposite happened. With Bell sitting in the press box rooting against his team, Jim Plunkett hit Randy Vataha for an 88-yard touchdown with two minutes left to seal a 21-17 Pats upset.

"The defensive back fell down, and I ran down the sideline knowing we were about to beat the world-champion Baltimore Colts," said Vataha. "What a great moment in Patriots history, right? Later I heard the general manager was in the press box cursing and swearing at me as I ran down the field: 'Go down, you stupid fool!'"

Bell is still amazed by the outcome three decades after the fact.

"Can you believe it?" he asked. "Billy Sullivan was in front of the cameras the second we landed back in Boston talking about Mazur returning as coach. And then the next year went down just as I had predicted."

Indeed, the 1972 Pats lost 10 of their last 11 games to finish the season at 3-11. Mazur was out in November after a 52-0 loss in Miami. Bell was gone soon after.

"I remember Upton came down to the locker room and stood up in front of the team," said Vataha. "He said, 'I just want to let you all know I've let John Mazur go. We're going to hire a new coach, and this is going to be a new era of stability. We have a plan. We're going to implement the plan. We won the championship in Baltimore, and now we're going to win it in New England. I want you guys to feel confident we're on the right track.' And on and on.

"Then a few days later, we went to practice and Billy Sullivan came down and said, 'I just want to let you know I've fired Upton Bell—and we're going to have a new era of stability. We have a plan. We're going to implement the plan. I want you guys to feel we're on the right track.'

"And on and on."

BASHFUL

At five foot nine, Vataha wasn't much of a pro prospect, which explained why he wasn't drafted until the 17th round by the Los Angeles Rams in 1971. But his size did come in handy during one summer home from college, when Vataha landed a role playing one of the seven dwarfs at Disneyland in Anaheim, California.

Vataha was Bashful.

Vataha didn't make it with the Rams, but as a former Stanford teammate of the Pats' newly minted, No. 1 overall draft choice, Plunkett, Vataha had value in New England. Vataha was traded to the Pats late in the preseason and soon resumed his role as Plunkett's favorite target.

It turned out Bashful could play a little football, as Vataha lasted six seasons in New England and twice led the Pats in receiving (1971 and 1975).

Vataha would stay involved with the business of sports long after his playing days, working for famed sports agent Bob Wolf and later becoming a co-owner of the USFL Boston Breakers. Today, Vataha runs an investment banking firm that focuses on arranging financing for professional sports teams. He was a key player in the sale of the Boston Celtics in 2002.

But like many players before and after him, Vataha's business sense landed him in Billy Sullivan's doghouse. In 1975, Pats players had grown tired of playing without a signed collective bargaining agreement, which had expired the year before. So they voted to strike for the team's final preseason game against the Jets. As the team's union representative, Vataha had to execute that order. The only problem was that the Patriots were the only team in the league who decided to take the action.

That's right. It was a one-team strike.

"That Saturday morning I was the one who had to go on the bus and tell [president] Chuck Sullivan we wouldn't be going to the game," said Vataha. "Everything just went wild. Billy called me and told me we couldn't do this. Pete Rozelle called and tried to talk me out of it. We went out on strike and it ended up being the first time a scheduled NFL game wasn't played. People just rolled their eyes. Only the Patriots."

THE BAY STATE PATRIOTS

How did the "Boston" Patriots become the "New England" Patriots?

Bell said it was his idea, and in researching this book we couldn't find anyone to dispute that claim. So for the sake of history, the credit goes to Bell.

After being rejected by the Boston city council a final time on a new stadium in 1970, Pat Sullivan said his father wanted to extract some revenge on the city by taking the "Boston" out of the Patriots. And with the new stadium going up in suburban Foxboro, Sullivan wanted the name to have more of a regional influence.

So early in 1971, the team became the "Bay State" Patriots. A press conference was called and a banner unfurled. Unfortunately, the newspapers had to abbreviate the name to fit it into headlines, and soon fans were snickering at the "BS" Patriots.

"The first day I came here for my press conference I picked up one of the papers and right there on the front page it said, 'BS Patriots to hire Bell,'" said Bell. "Every writer in town was having a field day. The bullshit Patriots. So one of my first moves was to ask Billy if we could change the name to the 'New England' Patriots. I didn't want to tell Billy that, hey, we look ridiculous.

"The board eventually agreed."

The Bay State Patriots officially became the New England Patriots on March 22, 1971.

3

THE SPIRIT
OF '76

In the upside-down world of the Patriots, it's only fitting that arguably the most talented team in franchise history never won a playoff game.

That's right. If you're going to rank the greatest Patriots teams of all time, be prepared for an argument from the '70s set. Forget the Super Bowl champions of 2001 and 2003. Forget the Super Bowl finalists of 1985 and 1996. Ask fans of a certain generation, and they'll insist the Patriots from 1976-78 were the best ever—even though they never tasted postseason glory.

"People go crazy when I say this, but even considering what they've done under Bill Belichick, I still believe that in terms of pure talent, the 1976 team was probably the best that was ever on the field for the Patriots," said Patrick Sullivan. "In terms of what was accomplished, it obviously wasn't as good as the championship teams, or even the one that went to the Super Bowl in 1985. But if you go position by position and compare the rosters, you'll find yourself saying, 'This guy in '76 was a better player than the one in '01, and '03, and '85—and so was this guy, and so was that guy.' It was an unbelievable team."

Indeed, the lineup that coach Chuck Fairbanks put together would be virtually impossible to assemble today in the salary cap era. Guard John Hannah and cornerback Mike Haynes were the best players at their positions in the league, and both wound up in the Hall of

Fame. Tight end Russ Francis, tackle Leon Gray, running back Sam Cunningham, receiver Stanley Morgan, linebacker Steve Nelson, safety Tim Fox, and defensive end Julius Adams combined with Hannah and Haynes to play in 30 Pro Bowls. Steve Grogan, an unheralded fifth-round pick, was the heart-and-soul quarterback. Fairbanks was Bill Parcells two decades before the Tuna.

In three seasons from 1976 through 1978, the Pats had records of 11-3, 9-5 and 11-5, more than doubling their win total from the previous four years (15-41). They made the playoffs twice. In 1978, they ran over teams for a total of 3,165 rushing yards, a single-season NFL record that stands today. They had toughness, character, and boatloads of talent.

"It was absolutely the best Patriots team we ever had," said Hannah. "That was a great football team. It had heart. It worked hard. Guys led each other, and I could give you 100 examples. In the Oakland playoff game [in '76], George Atkinson popped his elbow through Russ Francis's facemask and broke his nose. Russ left the game because he didn't think he could play. So [linebacker] Steve Zabel came over, stuck his fingers in Russ's nose and popped it back into place. Then he said, 'Get your ass back out there,' and Russ went. That's the way we did things."

Francis, by the way, knows a thing or two about great teams, spending the final years of his career as a member of the Bill Walsh-Joe Montana dynasty in San Francisco. According to Francis, there was no difference between the Pats of the '70s and the 49ers of the '80s when it came to talent.

"If that Patriots team had been left alone, it would have been every bit as good as those San Francisco teams," said Francis. "I know that."

But the Pats weren't left alone, and that, sadly, explains why they never reached their full potential.

FAIRBANKS

By 1973, Billy Sullivan had a new stadium in Foxboro and new franchise quarterback in Jim Plunkett. What he didn't have was a legitimate, proven football man to run his operation. So after the 1972 debacle that featured the firings of Mazur and Bell and the interim hiring of former Green Bay bust Phil Bengston, Sullivan decided to pursue some of the biggest names in the sport. He nearly landed Penn State's Joe Paterno, who accepted the Pats job only to change his mind a few days later. Finally, Sullivan nabbed Chuck Fairbanks from the University of Oklahoma.

Fairbanks arrived in January in 1973 and immediately instilled a sense of competence. And to his credit, Sullivan gave Fairbanks personnel and organizational controls that no other Patriots coach had ever enjoyed.

Three years later, the Pats were a Super Bowl contender.

Fairbanks operated the team like a CEO, bringing in a stable of well-regarded coaches and giving them the power and freedom to run the team. In turn, Fairbanks spent his time and energy on acquiring the talent, and in that regard he proved to be brilliant. Like all great coaches before and after him, Fairbanks focused on finding football players who fit his system, not just athletes. Fairbanks required his college scouts to attend training camp every summer and shadow a specific position coach. Those scouts would then go out and try to find players who fit the coach's needs. At draft time, Fairbanks brought everyone together and made the final decisions. The results were resounding.

Like any great leader, Fairbanks wasn't afraid to make the big move. His biggest came in 1976, when he dealt quarterback Jim Plunkett to San Francisco for a package of draft picks that would be unattainable today—the 49ers' two first-round choices in 1976 and their first- and second-rounders in 1977. Out of that came center Pete Brock, cornerback Raymond Clayborn and Fox, all of them key contributors into the '80s. That trade (and others) gave Fairbanks 10 first-round picks over his six years in New England, a bounty that kept the team competitive for the next decade.

"Plunkett was the best and most accomplished player we had, but the fact was he could bring the most in return, and we didn't have a good team," said Fairbanks. "And the only reason I could make that trade was because we had drafted Grogan. So that made it possible for us get those draft picks. It's one of the reasons those drafts looked so good."

Fairbanks also had an eye for sideline talent, and one of his lasting legacies was the coaching staff he assembled in New England. Assistants like Hank Bullough, Ron Erhardt, Red Miller, Sam Rutigliano, Charlie Sumner, Ray Perkins, and Ray Berry all went on to become professional head coaches. Some weren't very good in the top job, but all were excellent under Fairbanks.

"Chuck just had enough confidence in himself to surround himself with people who knew more than he did," said Hannah.

Chuck Fairbanks led the Patriots to their first real success after the NFL-AFL merger. *(New England Patriots)*

To his players, Fairbanks was a hard, demanding coach, a precursor to what was to come decades later when Parcells and Bill Belichick whipped the Pats into shape.

"When you played for him you hated him," said Nelson. "You thought he had no personality. You thought he didn't have your best interest at heart. You thought he was everything he wasn't. But he was absolutely honest with us. He was tough. He treated everyone the same and it didn't matter if you were the starting quarterback or the 45th guy on the roster."

The starting quarterback agreed.

"Chuck was a guy you didn't want to cross," said Grogan. "He could come down on you pretty hard. He knew football, he knew how to motivate people around him and he had a great staff. But he was a guy that scared you a little bit."

Added kicker John Smith: "It seemed like he never spoke. He'd say about five words to me all year. Every camp he'd bring in two or three guys to kick against me, and by the third preseason game he would come up to me and say, 'John, I cut those guys. It's your job.' And that was it. I never heard from him the rest of the season."

When Fairbanks arrived in Foxboro, Pat Sullivan was cleaning offices as a member of the stadium maintenance crew. When Fairbanks left in 1978, one of the last things he told Billy Sullivan was that he should consider naming his son GM one day. That day arrived five years later.

"Fairbanks had a way of demanding the most out of you, and even though he really hosed my father [by leaving], I still feel to this day that he instilled a certain work ethic in me," said Sullivan. "As a coach, he dominated the players. He treated them like crap. In terms of the Xs and Os, he left that to his assistants, whom he used to goad into really big arguments among each other. I'd be cleaning the building and I'd walk by the staff meetings and the coaches would be screaming at each other. Just tearing each other apart. And Chuck wasn't even there.

"The players and I had an expression—the 'half-eye,'" added Sullivan. "Chuck had this habit that when you irritated him, which was often, he'd squint at you with one eye. If he was really irritated with you you'd get the 'double-half,' which was both eyes."

Nelson remembers it well.

"After we lost I made sure my head was down between my knees in the locker room," he said. "Because I didn't want to make eye contact with him."

OUTRAGE

Fairbanks didn't have to do much squinting in 1976, because that was the year his collection of individual talent came together to be a special team.

After a 5-3 start, the Pats won six straight games to close out the season and qualify for the postseason for the first time since the 1963 AFL championship. They were never really challenged past November 1, winning those six games by an average margin of 16 points. On the year, the Pats outscored teams by a whopping total of 376-236. Confidence was sky high as the Pats headed into their divisional playoff game at the Raiders, whom they had blown out, 48-17, in Foxboro in October.

But this time the game was in Oakland. This time, the game was refereed by Den Dreith. This time, the Pats would suffer the most devastating and controversial loss in franchise history.

Fairbanks called the Raiders' 24-21 win at Oakland-Alameda Coliseum a "tragedy," and the game still evokes outrage in New England. The players who were on the field that day can recall all the details. The name of Dreith remains cemented in New England sports infamy.

"I remember running off the field after that game," said Smith. "I was always the first guy in the locker room, but this time Steve Nelson ran right by me and—son of a gun—he went absolutely berserk in the locker room. He hit every gosh darn locker in the place. Smashing his helmet into things. Ranting and raving. Crazy. We had just gotten robbed, and I've never seen somebody so mad in my life. That was Steve Nelson after that game."

The passage of time has not made it any easier.

It took the Pats over 25 years to gain their revenge against the Raiders, when a controversial replay review reversed an apparent fumble by quarterback Tom Brady in a 2001 divisional playoff game at snowbound Foxboro Stadium. The Pats went on to win the Super Bowl and the Raiders haven't stopped complaining. But not even that turn of events has eased the pain.

"I had a lot of people come up to me after the 'tuck' game and tell me, 'You must feel vindicated,'" said Grogan. "Well, the fans may feel vindicated, but those of us who played in that game can never feel vindicated. We'll always feel like we got screwed."

Added Santos: "I remember at the Super Bowl, a guy from Oakland came up to me and said, 'You guys shouldn't be here.' And I said to him, 'Let me tell you something, pal. I was there in '76. What goes around comes around. Payback is a bitch. Too bad.'"

AN OFFSIDES AND AN INTERFERENCE

The Raiders entered the '76 game as prohibitive favorites, but it was the Pats who carried the play through three quarters. Short touchdown runs from Andy Johnson and Jess Phillips and a 26-yard touchdown pass from Grogan to Francis gave the Pats a commanding 21-10 lead heading into the final quarter.

The Raiders clawed back with a one-yard run by Mark Van Eagan early in the fourth, but the Pats were still in prime position to close out the game two possessions later when they drove into Oakland territory.

With under five minutes remaining and the Pats facing a second and eight from the Oakland 35-yard line, Cunningham took a handoff, found an opening to the outside and appeared to be headed for a sure first down. But at the last moment, he dipped out of bounds just in front of the first-down marker. Then, on third and one, the Pats jumped offsides (the rookie Brock, aligned as a third tight end, drew the flag). On the ensuing third and six, Grogan found Francis with a quick pass in the flat, but Francis couldn't get his hands on the ball because he was being held by Oakland's Phil Villapiano. The entire Pats bench (and everyone watching back home in New England) leapt up, looking for an interference call, but it never came. Smith then came up short on a 50-yard field goal attempt and the Raiders took over.

One more yard. One more first down. That's all the Pats needed to run out the clock and win the game.

"That was the number-one thing in that game," said center Bill Lenkaitis. "What in the hell is Cunningham doing going out of bounds? He's six foot four, 245 pounds. Atkinson broke Francis's nose with a forearm—so why don't you turn upfield and break their nose? What are you dancing for? Turn up field, get it by five yards, break Atkinson's nose and keep the clock running! It all comes back to that."

Added Bucko Kilroy: "Cunningham couldn't run for crap that day. That's what really hurt us, I say."

The blame for the next mistake was shared by many, most notably Grogan. Needing just a yard, Grogan decided to change the snap count from 'one' to 'three' in an attempt to draw the Raiders across the line. The maneuver produced the opposite effect.

"He went on three!" said Lenkaitis. "Grogan will probably tell you it was the dumbest thing he ever did. And it wasn't just Brock who jumped. It was Hog and Leon, too. You've got three guys on that left side who if someone hiccups in the stands they are going to take off. Why the hell not go 'first sound' and we'll knock the shit out of them? Instead we're going to fool them and go on three?"

Added Grogan: "I should have known better."

But if the Pats took responsibility for that turn of events, then they pointed the finger of blame squarely at the officials for blowing the pass interference on Francis.

"How bad was Villapiano holding me?" asked Francis, his voice rising. "How about hard enough to leave bruise marks on my arm. I remember turning to the side judge and he had his eyes up in the sky—like a little kid who didn't want to admit he'd done something wrong. It was so blatant that when I saw Phil at the Pro Bowl that year, he came right out and told me he had done it. He said, 'I was beat, so why not take the chance? It only would have been a first down, right? I can't believe they didn't throw a flag.'"

The non-call later brought out Francis's perverse sense of humor.

"I had Phil and his wife out to Hawaii one year and I had him on this little charter flight," said Francis. "Right in the middle of it I leaned over and opened up his door and tried to push him out. I got scratch marks all over my neck from his wife. She thought I was trying to kill him. I guess I was."

The play was hardly a laughing matter at the time, however.

"That was the biggest one," said Ray "Sugar Bear" Hamilton, who wound up suffering from that non-call more than anyone on the field. "It was just blatant. There was no way in the world that they can't call that pass interference—and they didn't. Anyone who knew a thing about football could have made that call."

Said Lenkaitis: "Russ couldn't even take his hands up from his groin because [Villapiano] had him completely pinned. The ball bounced off his shoulder, and the referee says that's a good play!? If any of that didn't happen, we never would have gotten to Ray Hamilton."

ROUGHING THE PASSER

After Smith's miss, the Raiders got the ball and drove deep into Pats territory. But, again, the game seemed to be in hand when Oakland's Ken Stabler dropped back on third and 18 and threw incomplete under heavy pressure from Hamilton. Hamilton actually tipped the ball as he bore in, and the ball sailed wildly toward the sidelines. The Pats then started walking back to the huddle to prepare for the Raiders' final, desperation play. That's when Dreith's yellow flag was spotted on the ground next to Stabler.

Roughing the passer on Hamilton. First down, Raiders. Five plays later, Stabler dove over the goal line with :10 on the clock and Oakland had the improbable victory.

Dreith always maintained it was the right call, but he's the only person outside of Oakland who felt that way. ESPN rated it as an honorable mention to the 10 worst calls ever made.

"It was a routine pass rush. I've hit the quarterback like that a million times," said Hamilton. "I hit him right on time. It was just a real terrible call. Real bad. Stabler sure wasn't saying anything. When I saw the flag I thought they had called holding on the Raiders. That's the only thing it could have been."

Added Fairbanks: "That was the weakest officiated game I've ever been a part of. They did a bad job. Terrible. I'll never forgive Ben Dreith for the call he made."

On the play, Hamilton grazed Stabler's helmet with his arm. Considering the league allowed far more contact with the quarterback in 1976 than it does today, the call was curious. Considering officials are supposed to let the players decide the big games in the crucial moments, the call was atrocious.

But Dreith never backed down.

"You bet. Roughing the passer," said Dreith. "He got a piece of the ball, but he [also] gave Stabler a kind of karate chop on the side of the head on the way down. ... I remember [the Pats] coaches chased us [after the game]. The only guy who didn't do anything was Fairbanks."

Replied Sullivan: "It's still irritating to this point. Just look at the tape, buddy!"

Hamilton was so irate that he was flagged twice for unsportsmanlike conduct as the Raiders continued their drive. He was ejected by Dreith after the Raiders' winning touchdown.

Hamilton is now a successful defensive line coach with the Jacksonville Jaguars. He's been an NFL assistant for over two decades and even spent two stints on the sidelines with the Pats (1985-89 and 1997-99). By any measure, he's put a lifetime between Ben Dreith's flag and where he is today. But, unfortunately for Hamilton, the past is never far away when it comes to Boston and sports. Hamilton said any conversation he has with a New Englander invariably goes back to one thing: Roughing the passer.

"I've learned to live with it now," said Hamilton. "It was obviously a big, big thing in Patriots history, but I thought there were a lot of other things in that game besides that. Everyone focuses on the roughing call. I'm used to it now, because the people in New England, even though they've won two Super Bowls, they still don't let it go.... It's like that Bill Buckner deal."

A LEVEL PLAYING FIELD?

Some Patriots players felt there was a higher power at work that day in Oakland. In other words, they thought the game was fixed.

"Absolutely," said Hannah. "I think there have been several games that have been fixed in the NFL, and that one was the most flagrant of them all. The NFL wanted the Raiders to get a new stadium in

Oakland. The league didn't want them to move. They thought if the Raiders won it all, they'd have a better chance of staying."

Added Francis: "I just can't say that [it was fixed]. But that was the only game I played in during my 14 years in the league where I felt something was wrong. There had to be something there. Could it be that the referees had a personal stake in the outcome somewhere down the line? Could it be that they were just that inept? I don't know. All I know is that I've played hundreds and hundreds of games, and that's the one that sticks out."

Hannah even believed there was something fishy on Cunningham's ill-fated run.

"The guy holding the first-down marker on the sidelines purposely held the sticks back so Sam wouldn't get the first down. He held them at least a yard in front of the actual first down. Sam used to run looking for the yard marker, that's how he ran, and the guy on the sidelines faked him out."

There was more. While the Raiders were actually flagged for more penalties than the Patriots (11 to 10), the Pats were the recipient of several questionable holding calls through the game. Lenkaitis, who didn't take a single holding call during the regular season, was flagged three times in Oakland. And the same sideline official who failed to penalize Atkinson for smashing Francis in the facemask also kept his flag in his pocket on the Villapiano interference.

"There's no doubt it was [fixed]," said Hamilton. "A couple times in the second half we had some quick-hitting plays that Sam Cunningham gained like 15-20 yards on. Plays where you didn't even have time to blink, never mind hold somebody. And they called three of those back, which was just a killer. What was behind it? You hear about the officials. You hear about Al Davis. But no one knows for sure. It's all speculation. There was just some weird stuff that went on in that game that allowed them to win."

But while no one was happy with the officiating, not everyone felt the game was rigged.

"I think in the immediate aftermath there was a lot of speculation about it, but as I've seen the film and watched the highlights, I don't think there was a conspiracy or anything like that," said Grogan. "There were a lot of marginal calls that all went against us, but we were just as much at fault as the referees were."

Steve Nelson and Steve Grogan have their opinions about the 1976 playoff loss to Oakland. *(New England Patriots)*

Added Lenkaitis: "They certainly wanted Oakland to win, and you can sit there and kill yourself over all the things that happened. But the truth is we killed ourselves."

And the roughing call? Nelson, for one, had this objective opinion:

"If Hamilton did that today it would absolutely be called," said Nelson. "Without a doubt. He hit him high. But back in '76, and the way that game was being played, with Atkinson breaking Francis's nose and all that, it wasn't anywhere close. I think Ben Dreith was a disgrace as a referee, but I don't think there was anything fixed about the game. I could have made a play on Stabler down on the goal line. We all had a part in it, and I had as much to do with it as anyone."

Pat Sullivan said there was only one thing about the game that was truly fixed.

"There was an incredible drought in California at that time," he said. "And I remember when we got out there the state was telling people to put bricks in their toilets, take one-minute showers, things like that. But when we walked out on the field, the grass had to be four inches long and was soaking wet. Absolutely soaking wet. We were the much faster team that year, all around, at every key position. And there was no question that the field had been soaked to slow the game down. No question.

"Now, do I think anything was organized about all those calls? No, I don't. The only thing that was definitely organized was the field. Today, something like that would never happen because the NFL takes total control over that. It was a typical, old-style tactic."

The Raiders were never threatened the rest of the playoffs, beating an injury-riddled Pittsburgh team by 17 points in the AFC Championship and an overmatched Minnesota team by 18 points in the Super Bowl. Oakland finished the year with just one loss, and Patriots fans were quick to remind everyone it came in Foxboro and it wasn't even close.

Today, the consensus in New England remains the same: the 1976 team should have been the franchise's first Super Bowl champion.

THE GOOD DOCTOR

If the Patriots of the mid-'70s ever had a loose tooth, they knew who to look for in the huddle.

Bill Lenkaitis came to the Pats via the San Diego Chargers in 1971, and by 1973 he was firmly ensconced as the starting center on one of the best offensive lines in football. He was also on his way to a degree in dentistry from the University of Tennessee, and in 1976 he assumed a double life as an NFL center by day and a practicing dentist by night.

In a typical week during the season, Lenkaitis would see patients for around five hours on Tuesdays, the players' day off, and for another couple hours on Thursdays after a full day of practice and meetings at Schaefer Stadium. In the off season, he expanded his hours.

"A lot of times I'd come off to the sidelines and see that someone had gotten whacked—and I'd have to look up their mouth," said Lenkaitis. "And it was either, 'You'll be fine.' Or, 'Come see me tomorrow.' I had to see [linebacker] George Webster one time. He had gotten whacked the day before. They got a picture of it in People magazine—me looking up George's mouth."

Lenkaitis was just another character on a team loaded with as much personality as talent.

"I can tell you we got along great. It was one for all and all for one," said Lenkaitis. "We just thoroughly enjoyed each other. Me and Jess Phillips would hook up and we'd 'three-piece' it up and head into New York City. Jess had a briefcase with a phone it. He was the first guy I ever saw, even on TV, who had a telephone in his brief case. He was like James Bond. And we'd go out and act like we were really something.

"Black, white or polka dot—it didn't matter," added Lenkaitis. "Leon Gray was a great guy. [Guard] Sam Adams was my roommate for eight or nine years. We all got along super. There weren't any assholes on that team."

THE ENGLISHMAN

The core of Fairbanks's team was acquired through the draft, but the kicker was a different story. A much different story.

A native of a small village in England, John Smith first came to America as a young university student who spent his summers in western Massachusetts teaching and working at a soccer camp. Smith was an accomplished soccer player back in Britain, and his plan was to turn professional at the end of his schooling. But in the summer of 1972, he was visiting relatives in New Jersey and preparing to fly home when he got a call from the director of his camp. The director wanted Smith to stop off at a field on his way to the airport and kick some footballs for a scout with the New York Jets.

Smith knew nothing about American football, and he had only kicked the oblong ball a few times at his camp in Massachusetts. But Smith had obviously put on a show, because his camp director was adamant. So Smith agreed, stopping off to kick a few field goals for the scout. Then he got on the plane and thought nothing of it. He was surprised when he got an offer from the scout to come back to New York for a full tryout. He declined.

"I told him that I didn't even know what a kicker does," said Smith. "I'd never seen a game. So I figured that was the end of it."

But word of Smith's powerful left leg circulated nonetheless. In May of 1973, an agent called him in Britain.

"It was a Tuesday," said Smith. "He said there's a ticket waiting for you at the airport for a flight to America on Thursday. Can you be here for a four-day tryout with the New England Patriots? I was getting married the next month, but I figured what the hell? A four-day holiday on the Yanks. I'll come over, eat some nice steaks, and go back. I had no intention of actually going through with it."

Smith arrived to find it was the Pats' first ever camp under Fairbanks.

"John Hannah, Sam Cunningham, and Darryl Stingley," said Smith. "Three No. 1 picks—and me."

Smith kicked well enough that weekend to be invited back for full training camp in July. That's when the fun really began.

"We were at UMass, and they had all these fields lined up next to each other," said Smith. "The first scrimmage was against the Redskins, and, naturally, I was way over on the far field, being the third or fourth kicker in camp. I was jogging around, playing with my soccer ball, when the equipment manager started shouting for me, 'Get over here! You're in, Smith! You're in for a field goal!' So I went racing over and jumped into the huddle. I came out, lined up, and kicked the field goal. Right down the middle. Thirty-six yards. My first field goal. I was tickled to death. I was jumping up and down, running to the sidelines. I'm a soccer player, remember. Fairbanks saw me and put up his finger, looking at me under that one eye like he would, beckoning. So I went over to him, excited. You know: 'Hey Coach, great kick, huh?'

"'Right,' he said. 'Where's your helmet?'

"I had forgotten it two fields over. I had gone out there without my helmet."

The Pats' first exhibition at the Hall of Fame game wasn't much better.

"The first game of football I ever saw was the one I was in," said Smith. "All I had to do was kick off for the second half. I had been kicking balls out of the end zone all camp, but this was the first time it was against real players in a game. So I lined up to discover this big linebacker standing 10 yards away shouting all sorts of abuse at my mother.

"I remember they told me to give a signal to the referee before I kicked, which I totally forgot to do. I took off early, and by the time I was halfway to the ball the players hadn't moved. The ref blew his whistle and brought me back. Try it again. So I lined up again and the only thing I could think about was that linebacker. I kicked it to about the 10-yard line and it just barely stayed in bounds. It was an awful kick. The game was on ABC with Howard Cosell. And he said something about me being a kid from England, and if I kept kicking like that I could expect a seat on the next boat back."

Smith wasn't on the next boat, but Fairbanks couldn't put him on the team until he learned the game. Smith was liable to hurt himself otherwise. So at the end of camp, the Pats traded Smith to the Steelers, who promptly waived him a week later. The Pats had the first claim and got Smith back. "I think the Irishmen had a deal," said Smith, referring to Billy Sullivan and Pittsburgh owner Art Rooney.

Smith spent that first year playing for the New England Colonials, a minor league team that shared Schaefer Stadium. And every Saturday,

Smith would make sure that he went to see a local college game. Smith learned the game, and in 1974 he beat out the competition to become the Pats' kicker, a job he held on and off for the next 10 years.

Smith remains in New England today, running the John Smith Soccer Center in Milford, Massachusetts. He has become a certifiable football junkie. American football, that is.

"I watch every single game that's on," said Smith. "Every one. The big college games, too. I go to them, I watch on television. It gets to the spring and I can't stand it. I pick up the papers and there's no football. I need it all the time.

"Crazy, huh?"

SEEDS OF DISCONTENT

As painfully as it ended, the Patriots' 1976 playoff season should have merely been a springboard. The roster was young and loaded. The coaching staff was top notch. The players believed they could beat any team in the league. Everything was set.

It's no exaggeration to say the Pats were on the verge of something great, and after 17 years of struggling for legitimacy, the organization finally had a chance to make its mark in New England. History had not been kind to the Pats, but this was their chance to reverse it.

Instead, they added to it.

It all began late in training camp in 1977, when Billy Sullivan and son Chuck wouldn't allow Fairbanks to re-sign Hannah and Gray to contract extensions the coach had worked out with the Pro Bowl linemen. The pair wound up holding out the first month of the regular season, and the Pats sputtered to a 2-2 start. Hannah and Gray returned in October, and the Pats won seven of their last 10 games, but it was too late. The Pats missed the playoffs by a game.

Beneath the surface, the situation had a devastating effect. The best player on the team, Hannah, became bitter and distrustful. Many of his teammates followed suit. And Fairbanks began to plan his exit strategy.

"It all happened a week before the season," recalled Fairbanks. "I had [agent] Howard Slusher at my home until the wee hours of the night working on these contracts. We finally hammered them out, but then Chuck Sullivan talked his dad into not honoring the commitment I had made that night."

It turned out to be a turning point in the history of the franchise.

"That was the end of it for me with the Patriots—right there," said Fairbanks. "I could no longer earn the faith and confidence of the players. I was the general manager and I had the authority to negotiate with those players, and the [Sullivans] reneged on the contract. That really upset the whole team. And it happened after we had made our final cuts in camp, so I had no replacements for those players. It was a bad deal. We played the year with two Pro Bowl players who were very unhappy. It was disruptive to the team, and it was sure disruptive to me."

By 1978 it was obvious that Fairbanks was angling for his departure. Players began to notice their coach associating with a particular group of out-of-town friends, both on road trips and at the office in Foxboro. One was an executive at Continental Airlines and a well-known booster at the University of Colorado. It didn't take long for the rumors to start swirling.

Naturally, the Sullivans didn't respond kindly to them.

"Billy Sullivan was relentless," said Gino Cappelletti, the team's radio broadcaster. "He would come to practice and constantly harass Fairbanks. He'd wait outside the locker room, wanting to sit down and talk to him, wanting him to admit he'd taken another job. Telling him you can't wear two hats, you can't serve two masters. Things like that, over and over. And Fairbanks just wouldn't own up to it. Billy could have said, let's just wait until the end of the year, but he couldn't let it go. It was his personality. He had to get Chuck to admit it, and it came at the expense of the team."

Still, the Pats were a physically dominant team, and they had too much talent to do anything but win football games. And that's exactly what they did, running over opponents en route to the NFL single-season rushing record (3,165 yards). One member of Fairbanks's staff remembers sitting in the film room at Sullivan Stadium a day after the Pats' 24-14 win over Philadelphia. Suddenly, the phone rang. On the other end was the Eagles' All-Pro linebacker Bill Bergey calling for Fairbanks. Puzzled, Fairbanks picked up the phone.

"I just had to call and tell you something," said Bergey. "That was the worst ass-whipping I ever had in the NFL."

The Pats eventually ran their record to 11-4 and were one win away from setting a franchise record for victories in a season when they headed to Miami for an appearance on Monday Night Football. They had already clinched a postseason berth and a coveted first-round bye. For the first time ever, the Pats would host a playoff game.

It was the high point of Patriots football.

CO-HEAD COACHES

The night before the Dolphins game, Fairbanks had dinner with Billy Sullivan in Miami and finally admitted what everyone already knew—that he intended to leave the Patriots at the end of the season to take another job. Fairbanks told Sullivan that he wanted to keep it out of the press and that he was committed to coaching the team as long as it remained in the playoffs. Fairbanks felt it was a reasonable enough position.

"It was all supposed to be done in private, and when the season was over we would move on," said Fairbanks. "But it didn't go down that way."

It didn't because Billy Sullivan wouldn't let it. And, as usual, Chuck Sullivan was there to push the legal remedies. The Pats weren't about to fire Fairbanks, because they would have been on the hook for the money they owed him for the remainder of his contract (he had a year left). And Fairbanks wasn't about to quit, because he would have lost the rights to that money.

So the Sullivans decided to suspend Fairbanks for the season finale, replacing him not with a single interim coach, but with "co-head coaches"—offensive coordinator Ron Erhardt and defensive coordinator Han Bullough.

Why two instead of one?

"It was my father's idea, because he felt both guys would be candidates for the head job the next year," said Pat Sullivan. "And he felt if he picked one over the other it would have been unfair to the other guy."

Billy Sullivan announced his intentions to a select group of players on Sunday night at the team hotel, but most players didn't know the full story until they got to the stadium on Monday. Fairbanks also showed up to the visitors locker room at the Orange Bowl ready to coach his team. That's when Billy Sullivan burst into the room and ordered Fairbanks out. Some reports claimed the confrontation was heated. One account even had Fairbanks being escorted out by police at gunpoint.

Fairbanks said none of that was true.

"I just walked out a back door," he said.

The players were then treated to two pregame speeches, two halftime speeches, and two postgame speeches from Erhardt and Bullough.

"It was like a debate," said Steve Nelson. "It was like an auditioning hour to become the next head coach. It was a joke."

Said Hannah: "Billy came in and announced that [Fairbanks was suspended], and we didn't give a rat's ass. We were ready to win the game. We all knew Chuck was leaving. That Continental Airlines guy was around all year. It was obvious—and we didn't really care. But then Billy starts ranting and raving like a banshee. We actually had three pregame speeches that night. Billy's was the third. He just called Fairbanks an asshole over and over. It was a farce."

Fans were mostly in the dark—until, that is, Howard Cosell came on the air and delivered the news in his inimitable fashion. Up in the radio booth, Gil Santos was as confused as anyone.

"They introduced the team, and then they introduced Bullough and Erhardt as co-head coaches!" said Santos. "That's when I found out. No one had any idea that was going on until they walked onto the field. No one knew what the hell was going on. The team was in turmoil. The coach was gone. Then you had two head coaches? Ridiculous."

Erhardt called the offensive plays and Bullough called the defensive signals. But, to this day, no one knows what would have happened if the Pats were in an onside kick situation late in the game. Or if they were faced with the decision to go for it on fourth down. Who would have made the call? Good question. As it turned out, those issues weren't relevant. The Pats were humiliated by the Dolphins in front of Cosell and the nation, 23-3.

THE FINAL ACT

The co-head coaches was a bad idea. But what happened next was worse: Sullivan actually brought Fairbanks back to coach in the playoffs. Just a week before, Sullivan had defiantly said Fairbanks couldn't "serve two masters." Now, he was back. The result was a predictably horrible 31-14 loss to the Houston Oilers at Schaefer Stadium. So much for the first home postseason game in franchise history.

"It affected everybody. It was like a bomb going off in the locker room," said a member of Sullivan's staff in summing up the situation.

"I remember the Wednesday Chuck came back. He walked into the staff meeting and was like, 'I'm back.' Every coach and every player was wondering what the hell was going on."

According to Pat Sullivan, the team forced Fairbanks back to the sidelines to strengthen its case in the pending legal fight. According to

Fairbanks, the Sullivans offered him a lucrative extension to turn down Colorado and remain in New England.

Either way, the entire episode was a mess, and it cost the Pats another legitimate shot at a Super Bowl. Fairbanks said the Pats lost against Houston because Grogan was banged up (which was true) and because the Oilers bolted out to a 21-0 first-half lead (also true). But what Fairbanks failed to mention was that he had lost the locker room after the upheaval in Miami.

"He came back and said, 'I'm the boss,'" said Nelson. "And we all knew he wasn't the boss. He didn't have that hold on us that he had the previous years, not with me, anyway. He was a lame-duck coach—to the ultimate degree. No matter what he said that week, everyone knew he wasn't coming back. And some players had some hard feelings about it."

Center Bill Lenkaitis was one of them.

"I had a bad thing for Fairbanks because he lied to me," said Lenkaitis. "He said, 'Link, old buddy, I'm with you guys until we win the Super Bowl. My only direction is to get us to the Super Bowl.' Meanwhile, I hear he was making $2,500 worth of phone calls to recruits from our offices. That's like 500 calls! And this guy is lying about how hard we're going to try and win the Super Bowl?"

Added Pat Sullivan: "It was brutal. As much as the players disliked Chuck for the way he treated them, they also had an incredible amount of respect for him. He was a key to the success of that team, and they wanted him to stay. That Houston game, it was like everyone was just sleep-walking."

Of course, had the Sullivans allowed Fairbanks to do his job back in training camp in 1977, none of the rest would have happened. It's a fact that Pat Sullivan still seems in denial about, because when he was asked why Fairbanks would want to leave such a young, successful team at the peak of its powers, he gave the following explanation:

"I think [Fairbanks] felt he had reached a point where he brought this team as far as he could," said Sullivan. "And I think his wife put a tremendous amount of pressure on him to leave. She was never very happy here. They were from Michigan. He was from there and then went to Oklahoma, and compared to those environments, New England was different. They didn't like the pressure."

Nice try, Pat.

"They took Chuck's authority from him and turned him into a liar," corrected Hannah. "That's what happened. And Chuck finally said he wasn't going to do that anymore. He wasn't going to be their patsy."

Francis said it all came down to Fairbanks's need to flee the over-the-top management style of Chuck Sullivan.

"Coach Fairbanks just said I'm not going to let this little piss-ant kid who doesn't know a thing about football tell me what's going on," said Francis. "Chuck Sullivan screwed up a real good football team."

Fairbanks confirmed that he left for one reason and one reason only—interference from Billy and Chuck Sullivan.

"I had made up my mind I was leaving," said Fairbanks. "And after I finally told Billy, Chuck got involved and it became a legal issue. It was a bad thing, and if I had to do it over again, I would have waited until the end of the season to tell them.

"I had no real desire to go to the University of Colorado—or any other place. It was just available. It wasn't like they were enticing me to leave the Patriots. I just knew I couldn't continue to deal with the type of outside influences I had to deal with in New England. We weren't doing the best things for the franchise. There was too much interference with the decision-making process, and I told Billy that on several occasions. I told him we can't run this team from Foxboro, Boston and New York [where Chuck Sullivan was]. We had to get together on the same page, but that wasn't happening."

Meanwhile, Fairbanks by the end was most certainly serving two masters. It just so happened that the Pats' coaching staff had to coach the Pro Bowl in Los Angeles that year, and Fairbanks was still technically the coach at the time. During a practice session at the L.A. Coliseum, players and coaches looked over to see Fairbanks chatting on the sidelines with a group of men, two of whom were clearly athletes. It turned out the group consisted of two assistant coaches who Fairbanks had already hired for his Colorado staff and a pair of young Buffalo recruits.

Two masters, indeed.

The matter was finally settled in court. Pat Sullivan said the Pats received a $1.2 million settlement. Newspaper accounts at the time put the figure at $200,000. Whatever. The bottom line was that the team went south the next three years under Erhardt, who apparently gave a better halftime speech than Bullough in Miami and was named to succeed Fairbanks. It would be seven more years until the Pats finally won that elusive first playoff game.

Fairbanks was never the same, either, failing to duplicate his team-building magic at Colorado or with the New Jersey Generals of the USFL. Today, he splits his time between his home in Michigan and the golf course in Scottsdale, Arizona. He does consulting work for Bill Parcells and the Dallas Cowboys. He's content and at peace, far removed from Chuck Sullivan and the New England Patriots.

4

INSPIRATION

Darryl Stingley is a rarity. He's a former professional athlete who said he was going to give back to his community, and then he went out and did it. He's a professional athlete who said he was going to go back to school and earn his degree, and then he went back and got it. Stingley is a rarity because he doesn't deal in empty promises.

Stingley was the possession threat in Chuck Fairbanks's ball-control offense, a lean, athletic receiver who would have put up big numbers if only the Patriots had thrown the ball more. Instead, he made the most of the few chances that came his way and blocked like crazy the rest of the time. Stats or no stats, Stingley was still a huge talent on a hugely talented team.

But that's not what made him special. What made Stingley special occurred 20 years after his rookie season, when he founded his own charitable foundation and began teaching troubled inner-city youths the life skills needed to survive off the street. Stingley called it his "rites of passage" program, and he centered it in the same west side of Chicago neighborhood where he grew up.

Stingley recruited from the elementary schools, where he would seek out the biggest troublemakers and the kids who needed the most help. Those who were accepted to the program then had to attend classes and workshops on the weekends. Stingley started with basic building blocks like personal hygiene and restaurant etiquette. There were more serious

49

topics like drug counseling and police relations. Stingley also liked to include something called "perceptions of the hip-hop generation," in which he counseled his students on just what the image-makers were trying to accomplish with the baggy pants and jewelry.

But Stingley's best work came in the streets. Literally.

"I really humbled them," said Stingley. "I'd take them to the block they lived on, and while their friends were laughing at them they'd pick up trash in the street. And I'd just tell them, 'They're laughing at you now, but you're showing respect to the community. And the elders and the people in that community know what you're doing, and therefore you'll come out the better person.'"

Of course, getting the kids to stay in school was a priority, and that was something Stingley could preach with authority. In 1991, at the age of 40, Stingley began correspondence courses at Purdue University to finish his degree. The next year, he was in West Lafayette, Indiana, to pick up his diploma.

"When I dealt with the kids, I didn't want to be hypocritical," said Stingley. "I couldn't tell them to stay in school when I hadn't done it myself."

Stingley's program has been on hiatus since 2002, when funding dropped and he was forced to restructure. But Stingley promises to be back in the streets as soon as he gets things in order. And remember, Stingley doesn't deal in empty promises.

In the meantime, Stingley lives his life. He and his common-law wife, Martine, live in a high-rise condominium in Chicago overlooking Lake Michigan. He's a season ticket holder for the Chicago Bulls and a frequent visitor to Soldier Field for Bears games. He keeps tabs on his three sons and their three very different lives.

The eldest, Hank, has been unable to overcome the trappings of the street, and he's currently serving time for violating his probation. "He's not a bad kid," said Stingley. "But as we say in Chicago—he got caught up."

John, a son from another relationship, chose an opposite path. He's a Chicago police officer.

And the youngest, Derek, took after his father. He's a defensive back/receiver for the Dallas Desperados of the Arena Football League. Derek has played in the league for nine years, and in 1998 he even earned a tryout with the New York Jets. But, like so many others, he had trouble picking up Bill Belichick's defense and was sent home.

Darryl Stingley graduated from Purdue University, strengthening his "stay in school" message. (*New England Patriots*)

Stingley, at 52, is a grandfather to seven children, and that's what brings him the most joy. Christmas is his favorite time, when all the kids pour into his condo. And during the holidays in 2003, Stingley found out that his next Christmas would be even more bountiful. He was told an eighth grandchild was on the way. Stingley was also told the due date: August 12.

AUGUST 12, 1978

"Imagine that," said Stingley. "August 12. Maybe that will be a rebirth for me, too."

Here's what you must understand about Darryl Stingley: He is not defined by his wheelchair. He is not defined by the forearm-to-helmet hit from Jack Tatum that left him paralyzed from the neck down during an exhibition game in Oakland on August 12, 1978.

That may have been the story for many years, but not any longer. Stingley is now defined by his family, his faith and the work he has done for others. He is defined by his peace of mind, something so few pro athletes get to enjoy once they're done playing.

"You live with something, at first it's a shock, but you eventually transform. And, for me, the transformation is complete," said Stingley. "I've learned to build a constructive life as I know it, from this vantage point, being in a chair. I make sure those kids see that adversity is not going to hold me back. I show them that I experience life. I don't run, I don't catch the ball. I certainly don't dance, although I've been known to get my chair out on the floor. I don't do those things, but I'm still out there.

"Life is what it is now. The only time when I get truly frustrated—and I'm trying to psyche myself up right now—is when it comes to holding the kids. When each one of my grandkids were born—those were some lean years for me. I mean, the oldest one, for 18 years I've never been able to hold him."

It took Stingley a long time to shake the demons, over 25 years of mental and physical work. He nearly died from a collapsed lung soon after the injury, but he's here now. And for those kids who choose to listen, for those kids who chose to consider what Stingley has gone through, there can be no more powerful example of not giving up on life.

"At first, you're almost like a beach ball, just floating around," said Stingley. "But then you get grounded. And then you realize it's about taking advantage of what you have and seeing things as an opportunity.

Stingley went after every ball thrown to him, but on August 12, 1978, it led to tragedy. *(New England Patriots)*

I've always said that God prepared me for my life, for this life. He prepared me to see my kids grow up and see their kids grow up. And that's what has happened. I've seen my kids give me eight grandkids. When I was on my death bed with a collapsed lung, ready to succumb to pneumonia. I came through it. How much of that did I do myself? None. But I humbled myself to pray and I had the willpower to fight. It was God who determined that I should continue to live. And for what purpose? I'm not sure if it's been determined. But my heart is still with trying to help the kids. I try to reach out to those people who think they want to quit in life."

Of course, Stingley could have quit on that high, floating pass from Steve Grogan at Oakland Alameda Coliseum. But it wasn't in his nature, so he went up for the meaningless pass in the meaningless game and was throttled by Tatum. Anyone who was there that day can recall in an instant the sick feeling in their stomach when Stingley didn't get up. The feeling in Grogan's stomach was worse than most.

"Preseason game. Slant route," said Grogan, slowly recalling the facts. "Someone flashed in the first lane. I waited until he came into the second lane. And the ball took off on me. Darryl went up for it, and in most instances in a preseason game like that the defensive back would have just knocked him to the ground. But this guy decided to hammer him and just caught him in an awkward position. I threw hundreds of balls like that before and probably hundreds like it after, and nothing happened. But this time it was the wrong place at the wrong time.

"It was a late hit, and the ball was over his head. Everyone could see that. It was launching and, in my opinion, unnecessary. But you can't turn the clock back. It happened. I felt terrible, and I still feel terrible about what happened."

THE RECOVERY

Grogan shouldn't feel that terrible, mostly because Stingley doesn't. Stingley can look back at the play and see it for what it was: A young quarterback throwing an errant pass, and a young receiver doing everything he could to come down with the ball. After all, Stingley didn't see many passes head his way, even in the preseason, and he had a habit of making every one count.

"I didn't know any better," said Stingley. "I'd dive and catch the ball in practice like that. I wanted to let them know, you throw the ball to me, I'm going to go up and get it. Because how else could I make my living without some numbers? Remember, we weren't a numbers team in terms of throwing the ball. We had two or three running backs who ran for like 800 yards a season. We controlled the ball, and I was a possession guy. I had to get that ball."

After the injury, Stingley struggled for a long time to find an equilibrium. He split with Martine. His oldest son fell deeper into trouble. He lashed out.

"I was in limbo," said Stingley. "I'm not sure I liked the idea of being Darryl Stingley. I guess I wasn't a nice guy to be around, even though I felt like I never did anything verbally."

Stingley said there was no definitive turning point for him. The calendar, perhaps. He got back together with his wife after a separation of nearly 10 years. He started going out in public, particularly to Bulls games. He went back to school. He started his foundation.

"I wish I could say there was one shinning moment. I guess I just got sick and tired of asking, 'Why?'" said Stingley. "Only after I was able to quit the pity party was I able to realize the opportunity I had been given. Be strong and fight it and never give up. That's what I did."

Still, Stingley has his moments.

"The game that I got hurt.... I remember, Coach Fairbanks's son used to follow me around. He was the white shadow before that show ever came out," he said. "He used to carry my helmet around. So I was coming out of the tunnel onto the field that day and he looked up and saw I still had my watch on. I guess I had forgotten to take it off. So I gave him the watch to hold. I never got it back.

"Years later, I was at some function for the Patriots and I was sitting next to Coach Fairbanks. At one point, he turned to me and said, 'You know, my boy still has your watch.'

"And I just let go. I lost it. One sentence took me all the way back."

People wonder how Stingley survives financially. That's a long story with a good ending. Just before Stingley flew out with the team for the exhibition game in Oakland, his agent, Jack Sands, came to terms with the Patriots on a five-year contract extension. The final documents weren't ready when it came time to travel, so the Pats told Stingley to go play the game and the contract would be waiting for him when he returned.

"I remember what I told him before he got on the plane," said Sands. "Don't sprain your ankle."

Once Stingley recovered he found the deal was off the table. It took months for the Pats and the NFL to come up with an injury settlement,

Despite his paralysis, Stingley still made it to the Patriots sideline from time to time. *(New England Patriots)*

and the Raiders even voted against one proposal. Initially, the funds were not adequate. Stingley and Sands prepared a lawsuit.

"We thought about turning around and suing everybody," said Stingley. "But where would I be now? Probably in litigation."

So Stingley accepted a settlement from the league, and matters steadily improved over the years. Stingley saw his stipend grow with each successive collective bargaining agreement between the league and the players. And even though ownership of the Pats changed hands from the Sullivans, to Victor Kiam to James Orthwein to Robert Kraft, Stingley has received a yearly "gift" from the team.

Now Stingley is taking in well over six figures a year while living in his million-dollar condo. He has incredible technology to help him through his day, including a pulley system that allows him to get out of bed, go to the bathroom, and maneuver around his condo without any assistance. He says his life is comfortable, even "charmed."

Stingley has some dexterity in his right arm, although he can't move his fingers on that hand. And he has feeling in his entire body. "Lay me down, I'll close my eyes and I can tell you where you're touching me," he said.

Stingley still rehabs. He trains. The halo that he was once forced to wear to support he head is long gone. He's actually quite strong from the neck up.

"I can compete," he said. "I wake up in the morning and it's the same thing, it's always fourth down and a yard to go."

He doesn't really think about his condition, and for the most part he considers his life normal. But that's impossible to do for very long, because the phone always rings.

"So what happens in 2003? It's the 25th anniversary of the hit," said Stingley, laughing. "Reporters from everywhere called and it was always: 'Darryl, how you feeling?' And I like, 'Man, I'd be feeling a lot better if you'd quit asking me about it!'"

JACK TATUM

It's a part of the story that just won't go away: Jack Tatum never came to see Stingley after the injury, and he hasn't said a word to him since.

It's even worse than that. Tatum has capitalized on the incident, writing books and cultivating an image that glorified the devastating hit. His Assassin books were reprehensible. One example: In *Final Confessions of NFL Assassin Jack Tatum*, Tatum criticized Deion Sanders for his lack of physical play. "If Deion was playing my position on August 12, 1978, Darryl Stingley wouldn't be confined to a wheelchair," wrote Tatum. "I was paid to hit, and the harder, the better."

Imagine this: Tatum has even tried to get Stingley to help promote the books, as his representatives have repeatedly attempted to get he and Stingley together for an on-air interview and reconciliation. Stingley has refused every time.

"If he wants to call or knock on my door, just him, that's fine," said Stingley. "But I'm not going to cheapen my story for a three-minute interview on television.

"It seems every time they get a black broadcaster they call me," added Stingley. "It started with James Brown and FOX. It was going to be 1996 in Dallas, and FOX was going to make a big donation to the foundation. Then we found out from my dear friend Will McDonough that Jack was doing it to promote his book. Then Deion Sanders called. CBS. Religious. It's Deion, so I'm supposed to jump up and down? The latest was Chris Carter. HBO. And he called right up until the last minute. 'Darryl let me come talk to you, man....'

"Carter did interview Jack, and his big penetrating question was, 'Did you try to go see Darryl in the hospital?' Jack said, 'Yeah.' And Chris was like, 'Did you bring anyone with you?' And he said, 'Well, no.' Cased closed. Jack never tried to come and see me. Everyone else did. John Madden. Dave Casper. I can't remember all the rest, but they came."

Sands said three people above all others distinguished themselves after the injury. The first was Madden, who continued to visit Stingley in the hospital for months. During one visit, Madden noticed that one of the machines attached to Stingley was malfunctioning, and his frantic call to the nurses may have saved Stingley's life. The second was receivers coach Ray Berry, who was one of the few who agreed to testify (had the case gone to trail) that Tatum's hit was malicious and done with intent to injure. And the third was tight end Russ Francis, who attached himself to Stingley's side whenever he returned to Boston.

Tatum ranks dead last on that list. And while Stingley may be at peace, he can still tell the difference between right and wrong. And Tatum has been about as wrong as a person can be over the years. In 1997, Tatum even had the gall to petition the NFL for $156,000 a year in benefits, citing the "mental anguish" he suffered since the hit.

"It's too bad he's taken the low road," said Stingley.

And then there's the ultimate irony: Tatum has begun to lose his limbs to diabetes. In 2003, Tatum had his left leg amputated below the knee, and unless further operations improved his condition, he was in danger of losing his legs and being confined to a wheelchair.

Everyone else would say, "What goes around comes around." But Stingley won't do that, because that would mean he has joined Tatum on the low road. That would mean he's hanging on, and Stingley got his life back because he let go. Stingley has moved on to a new and better place. It's not his fault that Tatum hasn't.

"Despite the obvious, I feel fortunate," said Stingley. "I see all these guys when they quit playing, they don't have any money. They don't have any purpose. They're lost. And I'm not. I have some bad days. But I go with it and thank God. I'm grateful for the opportunities. I actually played the game. I was in the arena. I always smile when I see the salaries today and the little routes they're running. I'd be all-world today. I played against bump-and-run. I had to fight to get open. It was like a boxing match to get open. But no regrets. No remorse. With me, all you'll see is that cat with the canary grin. I know what I could have done.

"This is life as I see it now from this wheelchair," he added. "What are my capabilities and what are my limitations? Well, let me maximize my abilities and forget about the rest. Let me do what's right for me and my family, do what's right in God's eye. Let me try to reach back to anybody who would be influenced by my name or my voice. Let me be grateful and be a shining example. Let me see that person who wants to quit in life. Let me talk to him.

"I mean, here I am. Right?"

5

HOG

To some, he is the greatest interior lineman in the history of the NFL. To others, he's the best player, at any position, they ever saw. Yes, John Hannah is arguably the greatest Patriots player of all time, but somehow that distinction doesn't quite do his career justice.

Taken with the fourth overall pick out of Alabama in 1973, Hannah was selected to the Pro Bowl in nine of his 13 seasons, a team record. He was selected as the NFL's offensive lineman of the year four consecutive seasons (1978-81). He missed only five games due to injury his entire career. He is currently the only career Patriot enshrined in the Pro Football Hall of Fame.

Physically, Hannah was imposing but not a specimen; his powerful legs and low center of gravity were simply perfect for the position he played. What truly set Hannah apart were his drive and tenacity. He was a devoted disciple of Paul "Bear" Bryant, and the second he showed up in Foxboro with his deep southern accent and ornery attitude everyone knew John Hannah was a different breed.

He was known merely as "Hog."

"After we drafted Hannah, we only had two losing seasons the next 13 years, so that should give you an idea what kind of player he was. And this was a guard we're talking about," said Bucko Kilroy, who ran the Pats scouting department in 1973. "We were criticized for drafting him so high, and people asked me what I was going to do with a short, little guard. And I said, 'Build an offensive line around him!' He was a dominating player. That's the only way to describe him. Dominating."

Said Fairbanks: "He had unbelievable speed and quickness for his size (six foot two, 265 pounds). And his flexibility was rare, which is so important for offensive linemen. He could bend down and put his elbows on the ground, and for a big man that was unusual.

"But more important than those physical attributes was the competitive heart that he had. He couldn't stand to get beat, individually or as a team. He competed so hard in every practice. I had a hard time getting him to let other players take snaps in practice. He wanted to take every turn, that's how badly he wanted to excel."

Hannah could be a one-man wrecking crew on sweeps, but he was at his best when he was allowed to simply fire out and hit the player across from him. Dolphins coach Don Shula said that's why he and other coaches routinely made sure their best defensive lineman was shifted to the other side of the line away from Hannah.

"That way at least our guy had a chance," said Shula.

Added Grogan: "He'd be responsible for blocking a linebacker on a certain play, and before you knew it the linebacker would be down, and without slowing down John would be out ahead taking out a cornerback. He'd get two or three guys on those sweeps like no one I've ever seen."

Hannah said his success was purely a matter of working harder than everyone else.

"Beauty is in the eye of the beholder," he said. "When I played I just wanted to make sure I left it all out there. I don't think I was a talented player. Coach Bryant instilled something in me, he said, 'John, you don't have that much talent, but if you work harder than everyone else you'll be better than everyone else.' And that's how I approached the game."

The result was devastating.

"I get into arguments about this all the time, but I think John Hannah was the greatest football player in the history of the game," said Pat Sullivan. "And they say, 'offensive lineman, right?' And I say, 'No. Football player.' I think he was the single greatest football player in the history of the game. He was the only offensive lineman that defenses had to have at least two guys account for. Or else he would just wreak havoc. That's how great he was. He was an incredible force on the field."

John Hannah *(Jim Mahoney/Boston Herald)*

GOOD SIDE?

When told that Pat Sullivan had called him the greatest football player ever, Hannah only grunted.

"He's just trying to get on my good side," he said.

Good side? Most of Hannah's teammates and coaches didn't know such a thing existed.

"He didn't speak to me until I made my first Pro Bowl," said Andre Tippett, who made his first trip to Hawaii after his third season. "I was in Honolulu, and he called me in my hotel room and said, 'I'm taking you to dinner. It's on Sullivan. Meet me in the lobby.' That was the first time he ever said a word to me."

Hannah's commitment to football was extraordinary, and he demanded that every single player on the team share that approach. Hannah had no use for those who didn't. Some teammates took that as a challenge and became better players. Others wilted.

"He was brutal on people," said Pat Sullivan. "Brutal. I remember one year Don Brocher [the team trainer] called me up in the office and said you've got to get down to the locker room—John is pitching a fit. So I got down there and John was throwing stuff all over the place. He was cursing like hell, saying, 'I can't believe this goddamn Pro Bowl voting. How in god's name could they vote [tackle] Brian Holloway to the Pro Bowl?' John was in the Pro Bowl himself, of course, but he was mad because he didn't think Holloway worked hard enough and therefore he didn't deserve to go. And this was a teammate! John said the only reason Brian got in was because of him.

"And I said, 'Of course that's why he's in, John. It's true. It's why Leon Gray was in for years. I could play next to you and I would probably make the Pro Bowl. Come on, John. Why don't you enjoy it?'"

While Hannah's teammates found him tough, most realized it was purely the result of trying to raise everyone's level of play—including his own.

"John was just better than everyone else, and he knew that and we knew that," said Grogan. "He wanted everyone to play to his level, which was hard for some guys to do. I don't think he ever did anything just for himself. He was a tough guy, he was an intense guy and he was probably the best player I ever played with. He did his job quietly, with a lot of intensity. But if you screwed up, he wasn't afraid to tell you.

John was a very opinionated guy who wasn't afraid to voice his opinion. That rubbed some people the wrong way and motivated others."

Young linemen like Trevor Matich (a first-round pick in 1985) crumbled under Hannah's pressure. Others like Pete Brock (a first-round pick in 1976) thrived under it.

"Me? Tough on my teammates? I don't think so," said Hannah without a hint of sarcasm. "Well, maybe Matich. He was a Tony Eason type. I expected my teammates to play tough, hard-nosed football. But I wasn't the only one who felt that way. Nelly played that way and so did Grogan. That's the way it's supposed to be! That's how you build a winner!"

Hannah was asked if the Patriots had enough of those players during his career.

"Sometimes we did, and sometimes we didn't," he said.

THE HOLDOUTS

Hannah is not only the greatest Patriots player of all time, he's also the angriest.

"I'm angry at the Sullivans," said Hannah. "Because I feel they didn't allow our team to win a Super Bowl championship. And that's the only real goal I ever had. I mean, the personal things that came to me were great, but they were a sub-goal. More than anything in my life I wanted a Super Bowl ring, and they kept it from me."

Of course, money was an obvious and constant problem between Hannah and the Sullivans. Their contract battles were legendary. But dismissing Hannah's bitterness as nothing more than a financial issue would be missing the big picture. Hannah had zero tolerance for being lied to. And he demanded that everyone around him have a commitment to excellence, not just his teammates.

On those counts, Hannah felt the Sullivans came up short.

"They never should have been in the league," said Hannah. "They never should have been in football. They weren't qualified. They had ill intent. They would lie, cheat and do anything they could."

Hannah still remembers that night in August of 1977 when he was awoken by a phone call in the middle of the night. It was his agent, Howard Slusher, who had just hammered out contract extensions for Hannah and Gray with Fairbanks. Hannah was told to get up and come meet with Billy and Chuck Sullivan to consummate the deal.

"I was making $40,000 in 1976, and Leon was making $38,500," said Hannah. "We had gone to the Pro Bowl the year before and the

Patriots had promised us both raises. We held out the last preseason game and then I got that call at 2 a.m. So we got over there, and Chuck Sullivan basically started crying on his dad's sleeve, saying, 'Oh, Daddy! You can't do this! You're going to bankrupt the team! Please, daddy!' And Billy went along with it. They told [Fairbanks] he had to renege on the deal."

Hannah and Gray sat out the first four games before an arbiter brokered a temporary settlement. Hannah said fellow NFL owners eventually put pressure on the Sullivans to sign the linemen to fair deals or risk losing them as free agents. "Sullivan ended up signing me for $165,000," said Hannah. "He probably could have had me for $135,000 before the season if he'd only done what he said he would."

Hannah held out again in 1983, but money was only part of the issue. Hannah despised coach Ron Meyer so much that he refused to report to training camp. Instead, Hannah stayed home in Alabama and contemplated going into the family business. "I thought, why put up with Ron Meyer when I can fall back on this and be set for the rest of my life?" said Hannah.

Hannah finally relented after Pat Sullivan made a trip down south with team psychiatrist Armand Nicholi.

"Pat said we'll take care of Ron Meyer and we'll make sure your next contract guarantees you'll never have to work again in your life," said Hannah. "And Nicholi is like, 'You've got to learn to trust people. John, you've got to trust.' So I came back. Of course, Meyer stayed. And when I signed my deal the next year it was nowhere near what they had promised it would be."

A NEW CHAPTER

Hannah's final season in 1985 was heroic. Playing with two balky shoulders and a badly damaged knee, Hannah set the tone up front as the Pats ran over opponents all the way to the Super Bowl. Of course, that game ended in disaster against the Bears.

Pats doctor Bert Zarins told Hannah during the season that there was no cartilage left in his knee and that his femur was beginning to deteriorate. Zarins's advice was to retire, so that's what Hannah did.

For the next decade he totally separated himself from the game of football, spending much of his time at his investment consulting firm.

"I couldn't be around football for years. It just ate at my guts that I wasn't playing," said Hannah. "I had to totally divorce myself from the game. It was the only way I could survive."

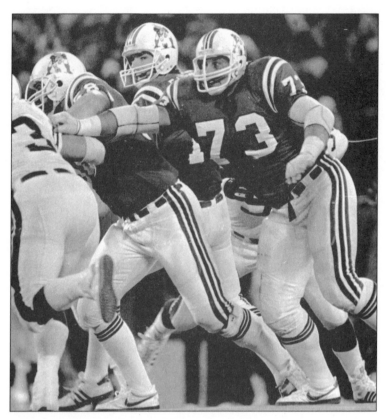

Hannah translated his off-the-field anger into on-the-field excellence. *(Jim Mahoney/Boston Herald)*

Hannah was drawn back to football when his stepson went out for the team at Governor Dummer Academy in Byfield, Massachusetts. Hannah surprised even himself when he volunteered to help coach.

"Little did I know that the love affair would begin all over again," said Hannah. "I enjoyed being around the boys, enjoyed instilling that attitude and seeing them go out and hit people. It's not about beating people. It's about going out and giving it all you've got."

That experience convinced Hannah to get back into the game on a full-time basis. He sent out letters and resumes to all 32 NFL teams. Only two responded. One was the Patriots, and in the spring of 2002, coach Bill Belichick drove up to Andover, Massachusetts, to have dinner with Hannah and discuss his career options.

"Belichick was really kind. He was a good guy," said Hannah. "He was going to let me do one of those NFL internships with him, where I'd come to camp and just observe and get involved on the fringe. I said I'd love to, but I didn't want to step on any toes. He said they'd talk it over—and I never heard back. Maybe [longtime assistant coach] Dante Scarnecchia remembered me chasing Ron Meyer around the stadium trying to kill him."

Eventually, Hannah accepted an offer to become head coach at Somerville High. The 2004 season was to be his first—at the age of 53.

Somerville's record in 2003 was 0-10. Did that phase Hannah?

"I went to the Patriots, didn't I?" he said. "It can't be any worse than that."

Hannah left Somerville at the end of the season.

As for his ill feelings towards the Sullivans and the Patriots, perhaps Hannah should consult with Nelson. His former teammate has some good advice.

"There's an old saying: You can't saw sawdust," said Nelson. "John's got to get on with his life. But that's Hog. I really like him. We played together 12 years and he's the best football player I ever saw. But he is stubborn."

6

THE '80s REVIVAL

It was a time of turmoil (what else was new?), but also a time when Patriots football finally arrived on the big stage in New England. The team that Chuck Fairbanks left behind should have accomplished great things in the 1980s. Instead, it stumbled around for half a decade before one final burst of glory.

The Patriots' Cinderella run to the Super Bowl in 1985 brought an outpouring of fan support that had been previously reserved for the Red Sox, Bruins and Celtics. And while the Pats slowly dipped back to the bottom of the league by the end of the decade, the '85 season was still powerful enough to keep the team relevant in New England until Robert Kraft took over in 1994.

The '80s were truly a case of hit or miss. The decade featured the Sullivans' greatest successes and most devastating failures. It was a time when they discovered the best football man in the family, Pat, while continuing to put too much trust (and money) in older brother Chuck.

Ultimately, it was a time when the Sullivans had to sell their beloved team.

And, hard as it was to believe, what came next was actually worse.

THE PLAYERS' COACH

It's a coaching progression so common it's become cliché:

The disciplinarian is tuned out by the locker room. A "players' coach" is brought in to relieve the tension and empower the veterans. The team falters, and soon there are whispers about a "lack of discipline." The players' coach is fired and replaced by a taskmaster, who is charged with whipping the team back into line. And on and on it goes.

The Patriots lived that cliché in the early '80s, as Sullivan settled on Ron Erhardt as the successor to Fairbanks. Erhardt was universally considered a good offensive coordinator and a nice guy. He got along with most everyone. The only problem was that he was not head coaching material. The Pats lit up the scoreboard during his tenure (the 441 points they scored in 1980 is still a team record), but they fell short of the postseason in each of his three seasons.

Erhardt's teams typically faded as the season wore on, losing four of their last six games in 1979 and four of their last seven games in 1980. They missed the playoffs by a game both years. The results indicated a team that wasn't strong enough, mentally or physically, to close the deal. And the power vacuum left by Fairbanks was obvious to everyone.

"Ron had a good football mind, but there was a lot of dissension on that team and he couldn't pull it all together," said cornerback Mike Haynes. "Chuck Fairbanks had the ability and the strength to make decisions. The players never had the feeling that Ron did. I remember at one point Ron got in front of the team and said that if there was anybody who didn't want to be a Patriot, they should come see him the next day. He said he was putting his foot down.

"The next day there was a line outside his office. Guys were tired of the dissension and tired of the losing."

The 1981 season proved to be a debacle, as the Pats found new and creative ways to lose every week, dropping their final nine games en route to a dead-last finish of 2-14. Erhardt was fired immediately after the season, with Billy Sullivan predictably saying that the team lacked discipline.

"If [Sullivan] thinks he can get a new coach to discipline this team simply by yelling and screaming at them, I feel he is mistaken," responded Erhardt. "What this team needs is more good players. I have been saying since I took over the job, that the cliché about this being the most talented team in the NFL is a joke."

Of course, like most Patriots coaches of that generation, Erhard was also victimized by a meddlesome owner, a disorganized front office and yearly contract battles involving the best players on the team. Most of it was beyond Erhardt's control. During the 1981 home finale against Buffalo, Sullivan reportedly burst into the coaches' booth and ordered quarterback Matt Cavanaugh benched in favor of Tom Owen. In 1979, in a move that demoralized the roster, All-Pro tackle Leon Gray was traded to Houston against the wishes of coaches and players. And the constant money fights ultimately led to trades involving marquee talents like Tim Fox, Russ Francis and Haynes.

Again, it went back to who called the shots. For most of his tenure, Fairbanks was that guy, and the players responded. Erhardt was never given that power by Sullivan, and the players responded to that, too.

"Ron didn't have the power to get rid of [players], and Chuck did," said Haynes. "If [Fairbanks] wanted to give you a raise, you got it. If he wanted to cut you, he did that, too."

The unraveling of the organization continued in the search for Erhardt's successor. The Pats initially set their sights on USC's John Robinson, with general manager Bucko Kilroy going so far as to tell reporters that the Pats had offered Robinson the job and were negotiating a contract. But unbeknownst to Kilroy, in a separate press briefing at virtually the same time, vice president Chuck Sullivan said the Pats had not offered the job to anyone. Kilroy was left scratching his head.

Robinson took one look at the situation and rejected the Pats' offer.

THE FRAUD

The chaos in New England didn't stop Ron Meyer from signing on the dotted line, though. The former SMU coach took the Pats job and immediately launched into his tough-talking, hard-ass cowboy routine. The only problem was that the players realized almost immediately that Meyer was all talk and no substance. The players eventually grew to despise him, although Meyer, obtuse until the end, never seemed to realize it.

"I would like to know exactly how many of my players were unhappy with me, because I didn't get that feeling from traveling with them and working with them every day," said Meyer upon his dismissal midway through the 1984 season. "I would just like to know how many there really were?"

How many? Try most everyone.

"He was the biggest joke I've ever been around in my life," said John Hannah. "He knew nothing about football. He was strictly a public relations guy. He was a liar. He was a fraud. I chased him around the stadium one time trying to kill him. He was degrading our coaching staff—I won't say what it was about, but I found out it was a lie. And the son of a bitch ran from me."

Added John Smith: "He was a complete idiot. He'd only go into special teams meetings. He had no idea about offense or defense. He tried to tell John Hannah he was finished, tried to tell Steve Grogan he was finished, tried to tell Stanley Morgan he was finished, tried to tell Steve Nelson he was finished. All those great players. As far as he was concerned, those players were on their last legs. Can you imagine? I mean, the guy was a complete idiot."

Even the Sullivans eventually recognized their mistake.

"He did not have the respect of the players, and at the end of the day they did not believe he knew about football," said Pat Sullivan, who was then the general manager. "He tried to portray this image as a taskmaster, but the players saw through it. I'm reluctant to call it an act—but that's the only word that comes to mind."

The players grew so disgusted with Meyer that Sullivan was forced to hold players-only meetings so grievances could be aired. Meyer took that as an affront, and to flex his muscles he fired defensive coordinator Rod Rust in October of 1984, a move that he did not have the authority to make.

"I was at a league meeting in New Orleans and I got a call from Kevin Mannix [of the *Boston Herald*] asking for my reaction to the firing of Rod Rust," recalled Sullivan. "I said, 'Excuse me? The firing of who?' Ron basically did that to trigger his own firing, and it worked. He was fired the next day."

Meyer's three-year record with the Pats wasn't all that bad—5-4 in 1982, 8-8 in 1983 and 5-3 at the time of his firing in 1984—but his removal was an absolute must for the sanity of everyone involved with the team.

Said linebacker Larry McGrew: "I'd say the first reaction of a lot of guys to the news was, 'Yahoo.'"

NELLY

Talk about fate. After the Pats were kicked out of Fenway Park by the Red Sox in 1968, the Sullivans found themselves with a set of bleachers they had no use for. Those bleachers used to sit in front of the

Three-time Pro Bowl linebacker Steve Nelson delivers one of his 1,776 crushing tackles. *(New England Patriots)*

Green Monster, but now they were homeless. So the Pats searched for buyers, ultimately shipping the seats out to tiny North Dakota State.

A few years later, an unheralded linebacker out of Minnesota by the name of Steve Nelson would enroll at ND State and play in front of those very stands.

It must have been destiny, because today Nelson stands as one of the most recognizable and popular ex-Patriots. He's also one heck of a football coach, turning the Curry College Colonels into one of the top Division III programs in the nation. Many fans know Nelson for his work as an analyst on local radio and television, but those who remember him from his playing days recall one of the most aggressive and steady defensive players ever to wear a Patriots' uniform.

A second-round pick by Fairbanks in 1974, Nelson was the focal point of the defense for most of his 14 years in the league. He was voted to three Pro Bowls (1981, 1985-86) and recorded over 100 tackles in a season nine times. In 1984, he was credited with a whopping 204 tackles. Nelson was tough and durable, and in 1993 he was a shoo-in selection to the Patriots Hall of Fame.

Most of all, Nelson was a fixture through all of the Patriots' ups and downs. Always giving 100 percent on the field and acting with total class off it, Nelson was a proud constant in a sea of turmoil.

"The thing I'm most proud of is that I played my whole career with one team," said Nelson. "I started my first game as a rookie, and I started my last game as a 14-year veteran. And, in between, I started every game that I suited up for with the exception of one—and I had a broken arm. I still came off the bench in that one."

THE LEGEND

As a player, Raymond Berry was famous for his meticulousness. He was known to bring his own scale on the road, just to make sure he always played at his preferred weight, 182 pounds. He kept a cigar box filled with index cards on the sidelines, each containing pointers about plays and formations. He was as precise and exact as the patterns he ran for Colts quarterback Johnny Unitas.

One of Berry's legs was shorter than the other and his eyes were sensitive to light, yet his work ethic eventually carried him into the Pro Football Hall of Fame. Berry's defining moment came in the game that put the NFL on the map, catching 12 passes for 194 yards and a touchdown in the Colts' 23-17 overtime victory over the Giants in the 1958 championship.

Berry was your typical mild-mannered assistant when he joined Chuck Fairbanks's staff as receivers coach in 1978, and he remained in that capacity until he was fired along with the rest of Erhardt's coaches in 1981. Berry then went into civilian life, and in 1984 he was working for his brother-in-law out of his Medfield, Massachusetts, home when Pat Sullivan showed up at his door.

Even though he had been out of football over two years and had never even been a coordinator, Berry accepted Sullivan's offer to take over for Meyer. It was something he did with mixed emotions.

"I was never that keen about being a head coach," said Berry. "You step into the bull's-eye and it's not a matter of if you're going to be run out of town, but when. I never really felt that was something I wanted to run into."

Berry eventually would be run out of town, but not before he led the Pats to the Super Bowl in 1985 and an AFC East title in 1986. It turned out that hiring Berry was one of the best moves the Sullivans ever made.

Today, Berry's players speak of him in revered tones. They tell of a quiet leader who was the perfect antidote to Meyer's bluster, someone who instilled confidence and calm. Berry was humble and self-deprecating, yet authoritative. And as a former player, he had an uncanny knack for knowing when to push and when to let up. Berry may have been a detail freak as a player, but as a coach he had a light touch.

"I loved that guy," said linebacker Andre Tippett. "I wish he had stayed with me my whole career. He understood how to get the most out of everybody. He knew how to push a guy harder than he'd ever been pushed, but then he knew when to pull back the reins. And I thought the big thing was that he was a former player, because only a former player would know those things. He was a guy who understood when to work and when to rest the horses."

Added Nelson: "Ray had real knowledge of how to keep players fresh. We never wasted any time. I think the best thing about him was the way he talked to the team. He included everyone and was very trusting. And I think that actually may have been one of his downfalls. He was, and is, just a really solid man—and he projected that while he was with us."

Ray "Sugar Bear" Hamilton broke into the NFL coaching ranks as a defensive line coach on Berry's staff.

"He coached the guys like they were men," said Hamilton. "He was not a yeller and screamer. He made the team feel very, very confident that they could win. Before we played Miami [in the '85 AFC title game], we couldn't practice for a few days because of the weather, and he just said, 'You guys know what you're doing. You don't need to practice. Just go out and do what you know how to do.' He put an air around the team that nothing bothered it. He made the game the important thing."

1985

Berry's influence didn't immediately reflect in the won-loss record, as the Pats went 4-4 the rest of the way in 1984 and missed the playoffs by a game at 9-7. Still, the relief in the organization was palpable. "Raymond Berry earned more respect in one day than Ron Meyer earned in three years," said running back Tony Collins.

That respect manifested itself in 1985.

The Pats started the season with a loss at Cleveland, after which Tippett tore up the visitor's locker room at Municipal Stadium as his stunned teammates watched. And after five games, the Pats were 2-3, which was the exact point when Steve Grogan took over for an injured Tony Eason and Berry told his players they were "right on track."

The Pats won six straight. Then Grogan got hurt, Eason came back, and the Pats earned a wild-card spot after winning three of their last four games to finish 11-5.

(Another electrocution story: After the playoff-clinching win over Cincinnati in the season finale, a group of fans ripped down the goal posts and carried them out on Route 1 next to the Stadium. The posts hit a hanging wire, and five fans were electrocuted. There were no fatalities).

The real magic began in the postseason, as the Pats became the first team in NFL history to make the Super Bowl with three straight road victories. First came a 26-14 win at the Jets, the Pats' first postseason triumph in franchise history. Then the Pats exorcized their demons, earning payback for the controversial 1976 heartbreaker against the Raiders with a 27-20 win in Los Angeles. Everyone remembers the decisive play: a third-quarter fumble recovery for a touchdown by rookie Jim Bowman on a Tony Franklin kickoff.

Finally, the Pats got the ultimate monkey off their back, winning a game in the Orange Bowl for the first time in 18 tries with a 31-14 demolition of the Dolphins in the AFC Championship game. It was a game those associated with the team remember more than any other.

Raymond Berry (*Jim Mahoney/Boston Herald*)

"Yeah. Miami. Finally," said Hamilton. "It seemed like a predestined deal."

Added Patrick Sullivan: "Whenever I was in Miami for business or a game or whatever, I'd drive by the Orange Bowl and say, 'We're not going anywhere until we win there.' To get that win in that venue, which was an impossible place to play, I would say that was definitely the game."

The players all felt it.

"Talk about clicking on all cylinders," said Tippett. "We were doing everything that winning teams do. Running the ball. Playing defense. And that game was just tremendous. It was 'Squish the Fish.' We had never won down there, but we just walked into the Orange Bowl and we weren't going to be denied."

The Pats pounded the ball on the ground that postseason, as Eason had to throw only 16 passes against the Jets, 14 against the Raiders and 12 against the Dolphins. Led by the backfield duo of Craig James and Tony Collins, the Pats racked up a whopping 510 rushing yards in the three playoff games, including 255 in Miami.

And, once again, everything seemed to come back to Hannah, who played on pure guts while battling through a litany of injuries. It proved to be his NFL swan song.

"To me, the most interesting thing about the '85 team is that the players realized, maybe for the first time, that they could be far more successful as a team than a bunch of individuals—and the key guy in that was John Hannah," said Pat Sullivan. "John was rough on people, and until Raymond was able to harness that, it was tough. John was a force, and in 1985 he became an incredibly positive force, and that's one of the big reasons we went to the Super Bowl. He was playing with every conceivable injury known to man that year."

Did Hannah consider that year as special as everyone else?

"Not really," said Hog. "We did some special things. It was fun. But it wasn't as cohesive a group. We didn't have the fire we did on those 1976-78 teams. I enjoyed those years better."

SUPER BOWL XX

Some of Hannah's sour taste was surely the result of what happened in the Super Bowl and its aftermath.

The Chicago Bears happened to be in the midst of one of the greatest seasons in NFL history in 1985, and the personality of that team had captured the attention of America. "The Super Bowl Shuffle." Jim

The magical playoff run ended with a brutal loss to the Bears in the Super Bowl. *(Jim Mahoney/Boston Herald)*

McMahon and his headbands. The Refrigerator. Sweetness. The Bears were all the rage.

Fans in New England had certainly rallied around the Pats, but it didn't compare to what was going on in Chicago. For those of you Patriots season-ticket holders who tried in vain to get Super Bowl tickets from the team in 2001 and 2003, consider this: The Patriots in

1985 were able to accommodate every single season-ticker holder (all 7,500 of them) with two Super Bowl seats apiece. Over 1,200 people declined.

As for the game, the less said the better. It's a short tale.

The Pats recovered a fumble on the Bears' first play, kicked a field goal and then sat back as Chicago put up 44 unanswered points. The 46-10 final represented, to that point, the most lopsided result in Super Bowl history.

Eason's stat line—zero for six, three sacks—seemed to tell the story, but Berry had a different version.

"When I look back on that game, what I remember is our first offensive series," said Berry. "I had determined before the game that we were going to throw right out of the shoot. Because prior to that we had really been emphasizing the run, so we were going to do something different.

"On the first play, Tony put it right on the money to [tight end Lin] Dawson, but Dawson popped a knee tendon and fell to the ground. That would have been eight yards right there. On the second play, Stanley Morgan ran a slant and Tony put it on the money again, but [linebacker] Mike Singletary came over and got his hand in there and it went incomplete. Then on third and 10, Tony picked up the blitz perfectly and threw the hot read, which was a fade to Stephen Starring. Tony did the right thing, but Starling ran the wrong route and broke in. So Tony started the game zero for three, but he was dead-on perfect on all three throws."

After that, the floodgates opened.

"We couldn't protect the quarterback, and that was my fault," said Berry. "I couldn't come up with a system to handle the Bears' pass rush."

The only consolation for the Pats was that no else could come up with an answer for the Bears that year, either.

WHITE LIES

As if the embarrassing loss in the Super Bowl wasn't bad enough, the entire team was cast under a cloud two days later when the *Boston Globe* published a story claiming there was rampant drug use among players. Soon, six players were named as having tested positive for marijuana and cocaine at some point during the year—receiver Irving Fryar, defensive tackle Kenneth Sims, cornerback Raymond Clayborn, running back Tony Collins, defensive back Roland James, and Starring.

At first, Berry and Pat Sullivan confirmed many of the details in the story. Then the team backtracked. There were denials and clarifications. It got messy. Soon, only Collins seemed to be singled out. Two decades after the fact, those who played and coached on that team claim the drug issue was completely exaggerated, at least during the 1985 season.

"We had one guy who got put in the paper—Tony Collins—and that's all there was to it," said Hamilton. "With a doubt, all overblown."

Like many teams in all professional sports, the Pats DID have a drug problem in the early '80s, and it was probably at its worst when Berry took over in 1984. But Berry soon cracked down on it, and by 1985 many players had cleaned up or were addressing the issue through voluntary testing.

Pat Sullivan said in an interview for this book that no one tested positive during the '85 season. Revisionist history? Who knows? The bottom line is that Berry cared enough to tackle the problem. And after the Super Bowl the entire roster agreed to become the first NFL team to submit to team-wide testing.

"It was all about Raymond's effort to reach into people's lives and give them help," said Sullivan. "It went way beyond coaching, which tells you what kind of man Raymond was."

Whether the players were abusing drugs or not in 1985, it obviously didn't have an effect on the field. After all, the Pats made it all the way to the Super Bowl, where they lost only to a vastly superior team.

"Obviously, we did have a problem," said Berry. "But do you understand the real problem? The entire NFL had a bad drug problem. It was a league-wide thing, but, of course, no one wanted us to say that at the time."

One member of the organization during those years even went a step further.

"Here's the real irony," he said. "We were probably the cleanest team in the league that year. By that point we had it pretty well contained. I think we really had a edge on some teams that season. You could see it when we walked onto the field."

Internally, however, the damage had been done. Players were distrustful of their coach, their general manager, their teammates and the media. Who leaked the story? Who was using? It became an undercurrent in the locker room, and it was a tribute to Berry's leadership that the Patriots were able to claim the AFC East title in 1986 despite the swirling controversy.

The episode still left most players with a bad taste.

"We just didn't deserve that," said Nelson. "Yeah, we got blown out by the Bears. But we had such a good run, such a good season. And it really cast a suspicion over all of us."

Added Tippett: "That hurt everybody. I had two or three appearances set up after the Super Bowl that were pretty lucrative for me. But they called my agent and said because of this scandal we want to hold off—even though everyone knew my name wasn't on that list. I was pissed. And it caused dissension in the locker room. It wasn't so much in 1985, but afterwards. Because you have guys looking around and saying, 'You're the reason. No, you're the reason.' Everybody was pointing fingers. Everybody got mad at the media. But, hey, it was nobody's fault other than the guys that let it happen. Obviously, it was getting out of hand.

"You just didn't have the same loving feeling after that," added Tippett. "It was different. Guys were looking at each other funny. Pissed off. What should have been a great time became a totally different thing."

THE DOWNFALL

The decline after the 1985 Super Bowl season was slow and painful. The heart of the problem was personnel, as the Fairbanks holdovers were either traded or were forced into retirement—and the talent pool was never restocked. Most of the drafts from the 1980s were horrific. The Pats got Irving Fryar with the first selection in 1984, but nothing else. Center Trevor Matich was a first-round pick in 1985 and running back Reggie Dupard was the first selection in 1986. Neither came close to making an impact.

"We all know about the guys that didn't pan out," said Tippett. "We didn't continue to build on what we had. We had a bunch of guys who played together six or seven years, but I don't think we replenished the way we should have. It only a takes a couple of picks here or there to hurt you. One of those guys doesn't pan out, or there's an injury, and all of a sudden there's a third wheel out there."

The Patriots also suffered through some typical bad luck. In 1989, for instance, three key starters on defense—Tippett (torn pectoral), cornerback Ronnie Lippett (Achilles) and defensive end Garin Veris (knee)—were lost for season with injuries in the final preseason game against the Packers. Lippett went down in the third quarter, while Veris was hurt late in the second quarter.

Despite taking the Patriots to their first Super Bowl, Raymond Berry was fired by new owner Victor Kiam. *(Jim Mahoney/Boston Herald)*

Fans and media asked the same question: What were those players still doing in the game? Weren't starters supposed to be rested in the final preseason game?

In the past, Patriots players always felt like they were forced to play longer in exhibitions because the Sullivans felt more success in the preseason would mean more ticket sales come the regular season. But Tippett, for one, doesn't believe that was the motivation that fateful day in 1989.

"We were trying to re-establish ourselves because we had stumbled a bit the previous two years," said Tippett. "Now, the [Sullivans] would absolutely play us longer in the preseason for tickets—we knew that. But I don't think that's why we played longer in that game. Berry,

I think, was trying to show the public he was going to be a little bit tougher on us. He was demanding more of us that camp. So maybe that was all a part of it. I think if he had that crystal ball, none of us would have played that night. It was a fluke."

The Pats finished a predictable 5-11 in '89, and in the off-season new owner Victor Kiam demanded that Berry reorganize his coaching staff and relinquish most of his power. Berry refused and was fired. Of course, the situation was badly mismanaged, as Kiam and Pat Sullivan didn't get around to making the decision until February 26, which was too late to land a suitable replacement. Berry's successor ended up being defensive coordinator Rod Rust, the same man who had triggered Berry's hiring by being temporarily fired by Ron Meyer five years before.

Remember, everything on the Patriots goes in circles.

Berry did not leave as a popular coach among the fans, but history will look kindly on his tenure. He coached five and a half years and had only one losing season. He made the playoffs twice and the Super Bowl once. He guided the team through turbulent scandals and typical ownership upheavals. He brought dignity to the organization.

After leaving, Berry served brief stints as an assistant coach in Detroit and Denver. Today, he lives in Colorado and works as a public speaker and for a company that markets insurance products. He remembers his Patriots years fondly.

"When I think about those years, I can't help but think about my father, who was a Texas high school football coach," said Berry. "He was just this huge influence in my life. He was the best I've ever seen at building a team and getting it to believe in itself—as a team. And I had no idea that I had been programmed the same way—until I took over the Patriots."

Said Pat Sullivan: "In retrospect, I never should have fired Raymond. The team needed stability. It was probably the biggest mistake I ever made."

7

FOXBORO

When the bulldozers finally put Foxboro Stadium out of its misery in 2002, no one shed a tear, and the eulogies were short. After all, who wanted to remember toilets that wouldn't flush and traffic that wouldn't move? Who wanted to reminisce about aluminum bleachers and drunken melees? It wasn't like there was a winning tradition to revel in, either. This wasn't the Boston Garden we were talking about.

Rest in peace? Good riddance was more like it.

But while everyone was glad to see the stadium bite the dust after three decades of operation, those with a sense of history also recognized the facility for what it was:

The savior of the franchise.

After nearly a decade as nomads, the urgency to find a permanent home reached critical mass for the Pats in 1969. They had run out of options with the Red Sox and the local colleges, to the point where an early-season home game in 1968 had to be moved to Birmingham, Alabama, because of a conflict with the Sox. The post-merger NFL was pressuring the Sullivans to find a new stadium or move to a city that would build one. Rumors of a move were rampant. Proposals came and went. Finally, momentum seemed to be building for a stadium at Neponset Circle in Boston. There was only one problem.

"It basically came down to some of the boys in the council getting taken care of," said Pat Sullivan. "And my father said he wasn't going to 'take care' of anybody. So the votes weren't there."

The Pats then started talking to officials in Rockingham, N.H., where land next to a horse racing track would be given to the team and the Sullivans would be responsible for building the stadium. When *Quincy Patriot-Ledger* reporter Ron Hobson got wind of the deal, he went to his father, who did public relations for the Foxboro harness track, and suggested they do the same thing.

A deal was soon struck, and Schaefer Beer came aboard to put up 25 percent of the costs for naming rights. The Patriots finally had a home: Schaefer Stadium.

Construction was quick and cheap. In an era when teams in Pittsburgh, Philadelphia and Cincinnati were having huge, multipurpose stadiums built for them by their governments, the Pats were on their own. The result was a facility that cost $6.7 million and took just 327 days to build.

THIS IS THE NFL?

The finished product was hardly big time.

The location was one thing. Twenty-five miles south of Boston, Schaefer Stadium stood a few miles between a pair of expressways with just one road in, and one road out, of the main parking lots. It didn't take an urban planning genius to determine congestion on game days would be problematic. It was. The traffic jams were immediate and legendary.

The stadium itself wasn't much to look at, either. Half the stands were built on the side of a huge hole and the end zones weren't enclosed. The "concourses" were merely open spaces beneath the stands. The bathrooms, once they were finally finished, were small, cold, and dank.

The seating was similarly modest, with the vast majority of fans having to sit on aluminum bleachers that were rock cold in the winter and blazing hot in the sun. There were a few thousand chair-back seats for the more expensive locations down low, but most fans had to wrestle for position amid a nebulous sea of bodies. When attendance was down, it wasn't an issue. Otherwise, it was a mess.

Between the drinking and the jostling, fights became routine. Night games were particularly troublesome, and a Monday night game against the Jets in 1976 resulted in 63 arrests and 35 hospital visits, both NFL

Schaefer Stadium was the cheapest building in the NFL, and it was still overpriced. *(New England Patriots)*

records. Four years later, in a game that became known as "Monday Night Madness," police were forced to handcuff 56 fans to a chain-link fence because there weren't enough police vehicles to handle the crush. Two other fans were run over by cars. The police wound up writing arrest reports for charges ranging from malicious destruction of property to indecent exposure to assault and battery on a police officer. It wasn't exactly a family atmosphere.

The town of Foxboro eventually voted to ban night games, and the Pats didn't host a single prime-time game from 1981-95. Goodbye, Frank, Howard, and Dandy Don.

The players didn't have it much better. Compared to their previous homes, Schaefer constituted an upgrade. Compared to the rest of the league, it was barely adequate. Within a decade it was perhaps the worst stadium in the league. The locker rooms were cramped and poorly designed. There was never enough hot water. The weight room couldn't handle more than a dozen players at a time. The original artificial turf was hard as cement and, later, the natural grass surface turned into a mud bath in the rain.

It was common for players to see the stadium for the first time and say it reminded them of high school. Steve Grogan remembered walking into the tiny weight room for the first time and seeing just one bench press and one squat press for the entire team. Other players had different issues.

"I showed up thinking this was the big time," said receiver Randy Vataha. "So I went inside to use the urinal, and it was like five feet up on the wall. Now, I realize I was no giant, but no one could get up there. I had to stand on a box to go to the bathroom."

Vataha wasn't the only player who experienced similar problems. Baltimore's pint-sized halfback Don (the human bowling ball) Nottingham famously had to be held up by two teammates to use the facilities.

Said Vataha: "I just remember saying to myself: 'So this is the NFL?'"

The cramped locker rooms also led to some interesting "interactions" between the players and the media. The most famous example occurred in 1979, when reporters crowded around the locker of receiver Harold Jackson after a big game against the Jets. Surly cornerback Raymond Clayborn happened to have the locker next to Jackson, and when he tried to push his way through the crowd to get to his stall, he was met by hardscrabble *Boston Globe* columnist Will McDonough. McDonough told Clayborn to calm down. Clayborn told McDonough bleep-off and poked his finger at McDonough's chest. Unfortunately for Clayborn, his aim was bad and he drew contact near McDonough's eye. Without hesitating, the 43-year-old writer unleashed a right hook and sent the Pro Bowl defensive back tumbling into his locker stall. Clayborn got up and went back at McDonough. As the crowd surged back, Billy Sullivan, who liked to stand with the media and listen to his players after games, went tumbling into a large laundry hamper.

Reporters turned around to find the soles Sullivan's shoes staring at them from over the edge of the hamper.

THE GREAT FLUSH

It is perhaps the most famous Foxboro Stadium tale of them all. Pat Sullivan calls it, "Super Flush." Others call it "The Great Flush." Either way, the story has taken its rightful place in Patriots lore.

Schaefer was built on the highest point of land in Foxboro, a fact that was apparently overlooked by the designers of the plumbing system. The miscalculation was obvious during the first ever game at the stadium, an exhibition against the Giants on August 15, 1971, when there wasn't enough water pressure (or finished bathrooms) to handle the crush of 60,000 fans. Schaefer Beer was known as "The beer to have when you're having more than one," and fans that night obviously took the slogan to heart. The result was a cesspool of overflowing toilets that wouldn't flush.

One fan remembers going to the game as a young boy with his father and being scared out of his wits. Unsure of their surroundings, the father and son walked over a mile down Route 1, past abandoned cars on the side of the road, until they found the stadium. During the game, the pair entered a dark room beneath the stands to see fans urinating against a wall and another man defecating into a cardboard box. The young fan, Gerry Callahan, would grow up to cover the team as one of Boston's most prominent sportswriters.

The board of health was soon on the scene threatening to revoke the stadium's permit. Not only were the conditions unsanitary, but Foxboro officials feared that if a fire broke out somewhere in town on a Sunday afternoon, there wouldn't be enough water pressure to put it out.

So after building auxiliary water tanks next to the stadium and finishing the plumbing, the team was asked to perform a test. The Sullivans rounded up available family members, team and stadium employees and even some writers. They put a few people in every bathroom and handed out walkie-talkies. The plan was for everyone, at a signal, to run around and flush every toilet in their bathroom, thereby approximating the crush experienced during a typical halftime.

At the moment of truth, the word went out and the sound of flushing toilets filled the empty stadium.

"I was one of the 'flushees,'" said Hobson. "I had the urinals. Another guy had the toilets."

Said Gil Santos: "It was funny. We were all laughing like hell, saying, 'I can't believe I'm doing this.' First we turned on every faucet in every sink. Then we started flushing like crazy. To me, that's the funniest thing I can ever remember doing when it came to the Patriots."

The Pats passed the test and opening day was allowed to proceed as planned against Oakland on September 20, 1971.

To everyone's surprise, the Patriots wound up flush in victory, defeating the vaunted Raiders, 20-6.

Afterwards, the pipes burst in the Oakland locker room.

THE SNOWPLOW GAME

It was a nothing game in a forgotten, strike-shortened season, but when a prison inmate drove his snowplow onto the snow-bound Schaefer Stadium turf and cleared a spot for John Smith to kick a game-winning, 33-yard field goal against Miami, an all-time Foxboro Folly went into the history books. The 3-0 victory on December 12, 1982, kept the Pats alive for a berth in the expanded NFL playoffs, but that was always an afterthought.

The day before, there was a torrential December rainstorm, soaking the turf at Schaefer. At nightfall, the rain froze. Then, the next morning, it began to snow. Smith remembers waking up in his hotel room and thinking to himself, "beautiful." Most fans had the good sense to stay in their homes. The announced attendance was 25,716, but the actual number of bodies was far less.

When the players arrived at the stadium they found the field covered by six inches of snow on top of six inches of ice. No one could get their footing, and it became obvious early on that the game would go nowhere. Throwing the ball was nearly impossible (Grogan attempted only five passes all day), which left the teams to combine for 81 rushing attempts. Kicking was equally as treacherous, as Smith found out in the second quarter when the Pats drove to the Miami 1-yard line and coach Ron Meyer belatedly called for the field goal unit. The kick was from 18 yards out, closer than an extra point.

"Meyer, the idiot, took so long to make up his mind—'We're going to run it, no we're going to kick it. No we're going to run it.' And back and forth," said Smith. "By the time he shouted out, 'Field goal!' there was hardly any time left on the play clock. When I got out there Matt Cavanaugh, my holder, said, 'There's no time—just get back!' So I came into the ball, my leg went flying up in the air and I drove the ball right into John Hannah's butt."

Miami kicker Uwe Von Schamann also slipped badly on his one field goal attempt, sending another kick squarely into his line.

The game was scoreless going into the fourth quarter, when the Pats managed to run the ball deep into Miami territory. A timeout was called, and then Grogan had an idea.

All game, a guy on a snowplow had been driving onto the field sweeping snow off the yard lines. So during the timeout, Grogan, after a push from Meyer, ran over to the guy and told him to make a swerve

Say the phrase "Snowplow Game" to most Patriots and Dolphins fans, and you'll get very different reactions. *(New England Patriots)*

to where Smith and Cavanaugh were trying to clear out a spot. The driver dutifully followed directions.

"I was digging out my spot and all of a sudden this snow comes sweeping across my path, and across the spot where Matt had just cleared," said Smith. "And then I noticed the stupid snowplow. We were pissed. Matt said, 'We have to move! We have to move!' So that's all I remember. The stupid idiot was in my way. He got in Matt's way. He was sweeping snow onto where we were clearing it away. The snow wasn't the problem, it was the ice underneath. We had to start kicking at the ice all over again, and I never got a clear spot for my plant foot."

Tapes of the play clearly show Smith was able to kick off green space left from Henderson's maneuver. But Smith insisted his plant foot still landed on snow and ice, and if anything, the plow had messed him up.

"He didn't help me a bit," said Smith. "He didn't make a bit of difference."

Dolphins coach Don Shula was outraged—and he still is to this day.

"My immediate reaction at the time was that I wasn't quite sure what was going on," said Shula. "The referee was standing right there behind them. I mean, what was he thinking? The only thing I could have done, and I later second-guessed myself for not doing it, was throwing myself across the snowplow....But that would have cost us 15 yards and gotten them even closer."

The writers had a field day with the story, especially after they found out the snowplow driver was an inmate at nearby Norfolk Prison who was working the game as part of a work-release program arranged by Pat Sullivan. His name, Mark Henderson, is now known by two generations of Patriots fans.

"I remember going up to Henderson right after the kick," said Sullivan. "I told him, whatever you do, do not speak to the media about this. Sure enough, I turned a corner after the game and there was Henderson conducting a press conference. One of the Miami guys was all mad, and he asked Henderson, 'Do you realize that Coach Shula is the head of the competition committee?' And Henderson just looked at him and said, 'What's he going to do, throw me in jail?'"

Henderson did go back to prison that night.

As luck would have it, the Pats traveled to Miami for the playoffs the next month, and Dolphins owner Joe Robbie wasn't about to let the opportunity pass. He shipped in a huge mound of snow, which he placed in the open end zone at the Orange Bowl. Then he dressed a member of his ground crew in prison stripes and put him on a tractor. The fans roared. Smith went two for two in the sun and was booed lustily every time he came off the field. The Pats still lost, 28-13.

SULLIVAN/FOXBORO STADIUM

After gaining full control of the stadium for the first time in 1983, Billy Sullivan modestly renamed the facility after himself. He celebrated the birth of Sullivan Stadium with a free concert emceed by Howard Cosell and featuring the Boston Pops.

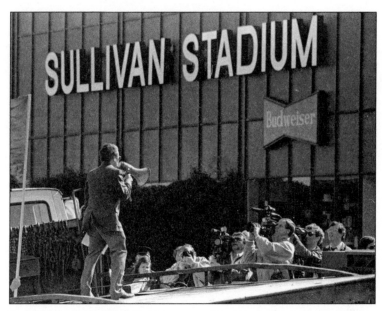

It's surprising that the Sullivans would want their name tied to the building. *(New England Patriots)*

The party did nothing to stem the growing tide of debt, and in 1991 Chuck Sullivan was forced to put the stadium into bankruptcy. Local businessman Robert Kraft snatched it up and renamed it Foxboro Stadium.

The name changes did absolutely nothing to improve conditions. And even though both the Sullivans and Kraft put in millions of dollars for upgrades, the stadium remained a woebegone facility.

"A lot of people thought of it as a hell hole," said Andre Tippett. "We saw other organizations and saw what they had, and it was easy to think the grass was greener on the other side."

Because it was.

But, to be fair, Foxboro Stadium had its moments. The atmosphere inside was outstanding when the building was full and the team was winning. The proximity of the stands, not to mention the heartiness of the fans, often gave the place a special feeling. The stadium had no "nosebleed" seats, and the players always said they felt like the crowd was right on top of them. If you forgot everything else—the traffic, the bathrooms, the bleachers and the drunks—it was actually a very good place to watch a game. And you couldn't beat the price.

The facility stood for over 30 years and accommodated millions upon millions of fans—and it didn't cost the taxpayers a single dime. And, most importantly, it kept the Patriots in New England.

"It's funny how people react to things," said Pat Sullivan. "Everybody said, 'Oh my God, the traffic, the toilets, everything is screwed up.' But wait a second. We just did something that no one else had to do. All our counterparts in the league were getting $50 million, $60 million stadiums built for them by the cities. Not us. We had to scrap that thing together ourselves."

And, ultimately, the players and fans survived. Just like the team.

"I've always contended that it wasn't your condo," said Bill Lenkaitis. "You didn't have to live there."

8

THE SULLIVANS

It didn't take an economics genius to figure out why owning the Patriots always seemed such an uphill battle for Billy Sullivan. He founded the team with $8,300 in his bank account.

What else do you need to know?

Unlike many of his fellow owners, Sullivan wasn't born with money and he didn't marry it, either. From the day he bought the franchise in 1959, Sullivan never had any financial breathing room. And because most every decision was ultimately based on money, the Pats wound up being the victim of hundreds of bad decisions. At times, the players and coaches were able to overcome them and win games. More often, the Pats collapsed under their weight.

But despite everything, despite all the blunders and missed opportunities, history should look kindly on the 30-year ownership of Billy Sullivan.

Because without him, without his determination and loyalty, the Boston area could very well be without NFL football today.

Sullivan had ample opportunity over the years to move the team or cash out. Had he done so, his financial problems probably would have been solved forever. Instead, he fought to keep the AFL alive in Boston and then survived the NFL waters in Foxboro. Remaining in New England cost him millions, but Sullivan was committed to keeping the Patriots a local institution.

For all his faults, Billy Sullivan did bring professional football to New England. *(Jim Mahoney/Boston Herald)*

So you can mock Sullivan and his team all you want. There's no shortage of material.

Just don't ignore his legacy.

BILLY

William H. Sullivan Jr. was the son of a Lowell, Massachusetts, newspaper reporter, one of five children who survived by working for as long he could remember. Sullivan eventually put himself through Boston College before embarking on his chosen vocation: public relations. He did PR for BC, the Boston Braves and, during World War II, the Navy. Later, Sullivan joined a local oil company and made a modest living. But when friend Frank Leahy called on behalf of the AFL, Sullivan found his true calling.

The fledging league must have been truly desperate for that eighth franchise, because Sullivan's finances, or lack thereof, should have scared away any clear-thinking enterprise. But Sullivan convinced the other AFL owners he could make it work, and he did. He and nine other friends/investors each put up $25,000 apiece and then sold public shares of non-voting stock to raise $500,000 in working capital.

The arrangement allowed Sullivan to get the franchise off the ground, but the partners and shareholders proved to be an albatross around his neck for three decades. In the early days, every major decision had to meet the approval of the board of directors. Later, there were warring factions and takeover bids. Sullivan actually lost control of the team in the '70s to Robert Marr, whose father, Dan, was an original partner who had saved Clive Rush from death by electrocution in 1970. (Remember, Patriots history goes in circles).

The younger Marr's coup d'etat was equally shocking, and Sullivan was able to get the team back only after his oldest son, Chuck, went deeper into debt to finance a takeover of the takeover. The stock that was sold to raise capital in the early '60s had to be bought back—at a huge cost. There were lawsuits on top of lawsuits, and Sullivan would eventually fight more battles in the courtroom than on the field.

The bottom line was this: Sullivan kept control of the team for most of his 30 years of ownership. He built a stadium. He had some fun. His team was even good every now and then.

Sullivan died of cancer at the age of 82 in 1998, a full decade after he was forced to sell his pride and joy. He was remembered as a true Boston character, a loquacious Irishman with a gregarious personality and a hot temper. He was a storyteller and a notorious note-writer.

Some said he would reply to thank you notes with thank you notes. He was fiercely loyal and held famous, life-long grudges. He was the eternal optimist.

To his coaches, Sullivan was meddlesome, a fact that scared away most of the good ones who came through the organization. To his players, Sullivan was cheap, a fact that led to yearly holdouts among the biggest stars on the team. In general, those charges had merit.

But, again, historians should look at those facts with perspective. Sullivan may not have been the perfect owner, but he was still the only one willing to take the risks and fight battles necessary to keep the Patriots afloat in Boston. Sullivan's story was one of perseverance, and fans in New England probably owe him more than they realize.

"I thought he was a courageous guy," said Larry Eisenhauer, a defensive end from the '60s. "He accomplished a lot just keeping the team in the city. He was there all the time. It became his career. It became his life. He was always so proud of the Patriots. After all of the pluses and minuses were added up, I think he was really an outstanding figure in this town when it came to sports. And I think he should be recognized as such."

Of course, everyone has their own memory of the Sullivan ownership.

"I remember the first game check I got," said Randy Vataha. "They used to give out the checks right after the game, and the next morning I had to go pick up a friend at the airport in Boston. So I went into the bank early, and I'll never forget it: 'Insufficient funds.' It wouldn't cash. They never thought someone would try and cash it so early. It cleared later that day, but you get the idea.

"I think Billy was a salesman, and I say that in a positive way," added Vataha. "You have to give him credit for the being the guy who stepped out when the AFL was a high-risk proposition as best."

Dozens of players found out through the years that Sullivan's affections changed dramatically once you entered the labor fray. In 1969, Sullivan traded linebacker Nick Buoniconti (the team's player representative) to Miami for a motley collection of players that included linebacker John Bramlett, quarterback Kim Hammond and a fifth-round draft choice. Bramlett and Hammond were gone inside of two years. Buoniconti went on to the Hall of Fame. It was an atrocious deal, and it was made purely because of the labor divide.

"At first I thought the [Sullivans] were really good people, then I became the player rep and everything changed," said defensive tackle

Houston Antwine. "Nick Buoniconti was the guy before me and they traded him—and we all know why that happened. Then when I became the rep, things with Billy really changed. I'd go places and hear that Billy had been 'downing' me in conversations. And I didn't think that was right."

Antwine said Sullivan would put such pressure on him that it got to the point where Antwine had to record their phone conversations. "I still have the tapes," said Antwine.

Steve Nelson always gave Sullivan the benefit of the doubt.

"Billy never, ever told me anything that didn't happen," said Nelson. "He never lied to me. Everything he said, he did.... I wasn't as combative as John Hannah was, but things still came up. The worst of it all came in 1987 when we went on strike, and the Sullivans were in a pinch. Mr. Sullivan was an older man and this was his life. And he would tell me and other veterans how disappointed he was in us. And we tried to tell him it wasn't a personal thing.

"But, overall, I really respected him," added Nelson. "I understood why he had to do some things. I can't say anything bad about him— nor would I."

Different coaches had different experiences. Chuck Fairbanks, of course, had one of the worst, as he constantly had to battle with interference from Billy in Boston and his son Chuck in New York.

"Billy was not a football type," said Fairbanks. "He was more on the public relations side. He had eternal optimism about the success of the franchise and he was always upbeat about what was going on. He was good to me in a lot of ways. But he was easily influenced by people who were not knowledgeable about the football side of the operation. He would have been better served if he had paid closer attention and had better lines of communication with the people he hired to run his business.

"He'd show up to the game with a bunch of his friends and be in a great mood," added Fairbanks. "And then afterwards, he'd ask you what was wrong with a certain player or why you did a certain thing. Well, maybe the guy was hurt and he didn't know it. Maybe there were legitimate reasons why things happened, and had he been better informed it would have been easier for him."

Raymond Berry felt fortunate that he got to work under Sullivan during one of the good times.

"The fact of the matter is that I was the head coach at the very best time of his ownership," said Berry. "He had delegated a lot of responsibility, mostly to Patrick, and Billy had probably made every mistake in the book by that point. So it turns out we got all the support we could have ever asked for. He didn't interfere. He was totally dedicated to winning. I couldn't have had a better owner."

Bucko Kilroy was among those who respected Sullivan for his determination to keep the team in New England.

"I think he was a great person," said Kilroy. "He had a chance to move this franchise to Jacksonville, where he would have had all his debts paid off. Plus a guaranteed sold-out stadium for five years. But he turned it down, just for his love of Boston.... He spent every dime he had on the franchise."

And in the end, that seems to be the prevailing opinion.

Said longtime radio announcer Gil Santos: "You just wish the guy had more money."

PAT

Is there another franchise in the history of professional sports where a janitor rose to become the team's general manager?

Only the Patriots.

Of course, Patrick Sullivan was more than just a janitor, he was Billy Sullivan's son, and he was a part of the Patriots from the very first day. He held nearly every job in the organization: ball boy, locker room attendant, PR assistant, head of the maintenance crew. Eventually, Pat was kicked upstairs as an assistant general manager. Then, in 1983—"after several nationwide searches," joked Pat—he became the team's GM.

Pat served in that capacity for nine years and enjoyed a level of success that was decent by NFL standards but excellent for the Patriots. In six of those nine years, the Pats finished at or above .500. They won their first ever postseason game. They made it to the Super Bowl. Sullivan was responsible for one brilliant coaching decision—hiring Raymond Berry in 1984—and two not-so-brilliant ones—hiring Rod Rust in 1990 and Dick MacPherson in 1991.

Through it all, Pat Sullivan was able to earn a measure of respect that the rest of his family didn't always enjoy. He was certainly a more level-headed and capable alternative to his older brother, Chuck. It was clear that after Pat took over in 1983, the organization just seemed more professional. In many ways, Pat was one of the best things to ever happen to the Patriots.

Pat Sullivan served the team in a number of roles. *(Jim Mahoney/Boston Herald)*

Pat Sullivan also understood the obvious financial realities of his family's ownership. Ask him any number of questions today about why the Patriots did this or that over the years, and he'll respond with the same one-word answer: "Money." For example: What was the problem between your family and John Hannah? Or: Why did you never replace the aluminum bleachers with regular seats? And, of course: How come you never won a Super Bowl?

"Money," said Pat. "Money, money, money."

Today, Pat Sullivan owns a successful company in New Hampshire that leases television production trucks, mostly for use at sporting events. Like everyone else, he is impressed with what the Pats have accomplished under Robert Kraft and Bill Belichick. But Pat is also quick to point out that his family's tenure was better than people think.

"In certain circles it was easy to say that during Bill Sullivan's ownership of the team, it was one disaster after another—and the facts just don't bear that out," he said. "If you just look at it statistically, from the time my father was truly the sole owner [from 1975-88], we had one of the best records in the league [116-94, with just two losing seasons]. So that perception bothered me, because my father's sole objective was to win."

HOW DOES IT FEEL TO
PLAY WITH THE BIG BOYS?

While Pat may have represented a departure from his family in some ways, he was still a Sullivan. And that meant he would fight, scrap, and claw for his team, regardless of the ramifications. The most famous example occurred after the Patriots' 1985 playoff win over the Raiders at the LA Coliseum, when Patrick got into a scuffle with a group of Raiders players as they headed into the locker room. Patrick wound up being clocked in the head by Raiders linebacker Matt Millen, a blow that left the GM bloodied but strangely satisfied.

"There was a lot of emotion built up into that one particular moment," said Sullivan, referring to a list of grievances the Patriots had against the Raiders at the time, including the 1976 playoff loss, the testimony of Al Davis against Billy Sullivan in a lawsuit that cost him millions, and, of course, the Darryl Stingley situation.

"And all the previous week there had been a lot of quotes in the paper, mostly from Howie Long, talking about what a lousy operation we had," added Sullivan. "So I was standing on the sidelines during the game and one of our assistant coaches happened to be riding Howie pretty good. Howie came over and thought I was the guy doing the talking, but I actually hadn't said a word all day. Of course, we were completely dominating them, so one time when Howie came over I said, 'You know, I'm not the one talking to you, but as long as you're here.... I didn't appreciate all that crap in the paper this week. And, by the way, maybe you ought to concentrate on playing, because you're getting your ass handed to you.'"

(Revisionist history alert: The Pats' performance was hardly dominant that day. They trailed 17-7 in the first half and won the game only because the Raiders turned the ball over six times. The Pats scored 20 of their 27 points off turnovers).

"So that sort of started the whole thing," continued Sullivan. "After the game, Howie and I got into it again and Millen saw the whole thing and that was that. He was protecting his teammate. He hit me from the side. Some said it was with his helmet, but I don't remember. All I remember was getting spun around, seeing him and thinking to myself, 'This is the single craziest man on the football field. What am I doing?'

"Inside the locker room, some reporter asked [team doctor] Burt Zarins if anyone was hurt from the game. And Burt just said, 'Aside from that goof Pat Sullivan, everyone is fine.'

Pat's mouth got him into trouble with the Raiders during the team's Super Bowl run. *(Jim Mahoney/Boston Herald)*

"I got eight stitches."

Long, a Hall of Fame defensive lineman, was from Boston and had. been upset with the Pats for not drafting him. He said that was his motivation for speaking up in the press. But, Long added, the only sparring he did was verbal.

"No punches thrown by me," said Long. "But Matt came from over the top of the turnbuckle and opened him up like a stuck pig. [Sullivan] said to me, 'Do you know who I am? ... I'm the owner of the Patriots.' And I said, 'Well, unless your old man died, you don't own anything.' That's when he grabbed me by the facemask, and then Millen clubbed him over the head—blood everywhere."

The story elicited a rare chuckle from Hannah.

"We were trying to tell Pat to keep his mouth shut—because the last thing you wanted to do was make Howie Long mad," said Hannah. "I was coming off the field with Nelly, Mike Haynes and my brother Charlie [a guard on the Raiders] and all of a sudden I saw this skirmish. Charlie jumped into it and started pounding on Pat, and I turned to Nelly and asked him if we should do anything. And, I swear it, Nelly said, 'He got himself into it, let him get himself out.' When I passed Pat in the locker room, with the doctor standing over him and blood everywhere, I just said, 'How does it feel to play with the big boys?'"

CHUCK, MICHAEL, AND THE VICTORY TOUR

Given all the debts and all the bad deals, it was only a matter of time until the Sullivans lost control of the Patriots for good. That time finally arrived in the mid-'80s, shortly after Chuck Sullivan's ill-advised deal with Michael Jackson to promote his family's 1984 Victory Tour. That's right. The ultimate undoing of Billy Sullivan's 30-year ownership of the Patriots proved to be Michael Jackson.

All together now: Only the Patriots.

Chuck was on the front lines of many of his father's battles, whether they were against players, coaches, shareholders, or whomever happened to be doing business with the Patriots. Unfortunately, Chuck had an aggressive style that often rubbed people the wrong way. The warm feelings that some people had for Billy did not extend to Chuck. And while Billy meddled with his team, Chuck meddled with his father. It was a deadly combination that derailed more than one promising season over the years.

"I always thought Chuck was a dork," said Bill Lenkaitis, summing up the opinion of many.

It seemed to be a well-earned reputation. One assistant coach remembers coming off the field after a huge come-from-behind win in Pittsburgh in September of 1976 and seeing something that told him all he needed to know about Chuck Sullivan. The Steelers had won the Super Bowl the year before, and the Pats were just beginning their rise under Fairbanks. In many ways, that victory in Pittsburgh put the Pats on the map.

"And when we got to the locker room there was Chuck Sullivan rubbing his hands together," said the coach. "He was saying, 'Boy are we going to sell some tickets now.' We were just like, 'What?'"

In fact, the Pats probably should have made their first charge in 1975, but they lost their first four games and never recovered en route to a 3-11 record. There was a reason. Thanks largely to the hardball negotiating tactics of Chuck Sullivan and his family, the Pats players went out on strike the day of their final preseason game. No other team in the NFL took the same action, but the Pats were so fed up that they threatened to carry out the strike into the regular season. The players stayed out Monday and Tuesday of the next week, with opening day looming on Sunday. The players finally relented late Wednesday, and Fairbanks held his first regular-season practice at midnight. Three days later, the Pats sleep-walked through a 7-0 defeat to Houston. The Pats never recovered until the next season.

Still, it was Chuck who saved the Patriots for his father in the '70s by engineering a costly and complicated takeover deal. It was also Chuck who brokered the settlement that gave his family sole ownership of Schaefer Stadium. The deals earned Chuck a reputation in some circles as a financial genius, particularly when it came to raising money. Months before stonewalling John Hannah and Leon Gray in '77, the NFL even made Chuck the chairman of the league's executive committee. Chuck once bailed Philadelphia Eagles owner Leonard Tose out of bankruptcy. He helped negotiate the league's "strike fund" during the players' 1982 walkout. He had his moments.

The Victory Tour was definitely not one of them. Chuck had done some music promotion throughout his life, booking bands at Boston College, helping run Bob Hope's RSO tour in Vietnam and arranging some acts at Sullivan Stadium. But the Jacksons? The idea sounded ridiculous from the start.

Chuck's business dealings with the Jacksons finally ended his family's ability to own the Patriots. *(Jim Mahoney/Boston Herald)*

Chuck saw it as an opportunity. So he signed a deal that guaranteed the Jacksons $41 million in revenue. Of course, Chuck had to borrow most of that money—and, ominously, he put up the stadium as collateral.

The tour tanked, mostly because the Jacksons wouldn't match Chuck's guarantee on revenue with a guarantee of their own on expenses. And the Jacksons' consumption on that tour became legendary, as every whim of Michael, Tito, and Jermaine was catered to. Chuck also miscalculated how many tickets he would be able to sell in many of the stadiums he had booked for the tour. Apparently, Chuck never realized that the Jacksons' huge stage setup would eliminate thousands of seats on the field. Chuck couldn't even get the Jacksons into his own stadium, as the Foxboro town board denied him a permit for the concerts.

It was a deal where nothing went right for Chuck. In hindsight, that made perfect sense, since the negotiating team representing the Jacksons included boxing promoter Don King and spiritual leader Al Sharpton.

"I remember saying to Chuck, 'Why are we getting into bed with Don King and Al Sharpton?'" said Pat. "How can we possibly win?"

They couldn't, but that didn't stop Chuck from throwing good money after bad. The next deal was a licensing contract that cost Chuck

$18 million for the rights to Michael Jackson merchandise and apparel. Unfortunately, almost immediately after the deal was signed, Jackson went into seclusion and started generating headlines for some truly bizarre behavior. In no time at all, Michael Jackson souvenirs weren't worth a dime and the team offices at Sullivan Stadium became home to truckloads of lunch boxes and T-shirts.

The stadium also became home to Chuck—literally. Apparently homeless, Chuck eventually set up a bedroom in one of the large "Super boxes" that overlooked the north end zone. Through the years, the room had been used as a working press area, and one day an unsuspecting reporter opened the door to the room to find a bed with rumpled sheets and clothes on the floor. He was quickly whisked away.

"It wasn't really the tour itself that was the killer," said Pat. "The tour lost about $2.5 million and we could have absorbed that fairly easily. The killer was the merchandising deal. That's what we couldn't recover from. We had trailers and trailers of stuff that just sat there."

No one knows exactly how much Chuck lost in the venture. Most estimates had the number at around $20 million.

"I don't know what the final number was," said Pat. "I just know it was a lot."

THE SALE

After the dust finally settled on the Victory Tour debacle, the Sullivan family found itself in massive debt, with some reports putting the hole at over $120 million. With interest rates rising and the team operating at a loss, it became impossible for the Sullivans to carry that debt. A massive shareholder lawsuit didn't help. The Sullivans had also sold an option to purchase the team to Philadelphia businessman Fran Murray. Soon, Murray was attempting to exercise that option, and the Sullivans were balking. More lawsuits followed.

The first to go was the stadium, which went into bankruptcy court and was purchased by Robert Kraft.

Then it got to the point where the Sullivans, particularly Chuck, were on the brink of personal bankruptcy. "And my father said he wasn't going to do that," said Pat. "He came from an old school that said bankruptcy was not a good thing. And if that meant he had to sell the team to pay off Chuck's debts, then that's what he was going to do."

So Sullivan's beloved team went on the market, and a long line of local and national businessmen came to Foxboro to kick the tires. The biggest name was real estate magnate Donald Trump, and he actually came close to completing the purchase. But the NFL, leery of Trump's casino holdings and his involvement in the ongoing USFL lawsuit, squashed the deal. Fans can only imagine how things would have turned out had The Donald bought the team. Talk about a reality series. ("Rod Rust....You're fired!").

"It was a very, very difficult period in my father's life, and in my bother's life and everyone in my family's life," said Pat. "But I think it's something we inevitably would have gone through one way or another because the taxes on my father's death would have been so enormous we would have had to sell the team, anyway."

Finally, on July 28, 1988, the Sullivans closed on an $84 million deal to sell to Remington shaver magnate Victor Kiam. Later, Billy Sullivan sued the NFL, which had denied him the right to sell more stock in the team through a public offering. The league had allowed the 49ers to do virtually the exact same thing, but by that time the NFL had apparently seen enough of the Sullivans.

Billy Sullivan eventually won his lawsuit and was awarded $141 million, a sum that was later reduced to $51 million. When the lawyers got through with it, the final number was $11.5 million. He didn't really care. After all the years and all the losses, Billy finally had a victory.

"He never really had any money anyway, so what difference did it make?" said Pat. "He was not a wealthy guy, and he never regarded that as the be-all and end-all. All he wanted to know was, are we successful at what we do? Are we enjoying it and are we doing things for other people? That's how he thought of things."

And on those counts, Billy Sullivan was a resounding success. If anyone doubts that, just look at cities like Baltimore and Cleveland, which lost far more successful and entrenched teams than the Patriots purely because of ownership greed.

Still, Pat Sullivan knows New England, and he knows Patriots fans. He knows his family will always be remembered a certain way by a certain number of people. It comes with the territory.

And nowhere is safe. Pat remembers going to a state prison to give a speech once, and when he got to the question-and-answer period, the first person to raise his hand was a giant, menacing inmate.

"He just stood up, stared right at me and said, 'Why the [expletive] did you guys trade Leon Gray?'" said Pat. "I guess that's the way it goes."

9

FROM PLUNKETT TO GROGAN TO EASON TO BLEDSOE

The first-rounders came with big names and big resumes. Steve Grogan and Tom Brady came with big hearts.

In the end, heart won out.

That's the *Reader's Digest* version of Patriots quarterbacking, as the four first-round picks in team history—Jack Concannon (1964), Jim Plunkett (1971), Tony Eason (1983) and Drew Bledsoe (1993)—all fell short of expectations. Meanwhile, Grogan, a fifth-round pick, became a cult hero, and Brady, a sixth-rounder, became a Super Bowl poster boy.

Plunkett was the first to fall. He was a Heisman Trophy winner and the first overall pick of the 1971 draft—and the Patriots didn't know what to do with him. He was a big, strong-armed pocket passer, but the Pats never built an offensive line to protect him or a system to take advantage of his talents. Plunkett was finally traded to San Francisco after taking a merciless, five-year pounding. In typical Patriots fashion, Plunkett later surfaced in Oakland and won two Super Bowls.

The Pats could afford to dump Plunkett after the 1975 season because of the emergence of Grogan, who was a dangerous pass-run threat with an old-school mentality. Grogan would suffer plenty of up and downs during his career, but he ultimately became one of the most popular players in team history after 16 years of black-and-blue service.

Eason came from Illinois with the 15th pick in 1983, arriving just as Grogan was suffering a mid-career dip. The opportunity was ripe for Eason to take the Pats into a new era, but he just wasn't tough enough to win over his teammates or the fans. Eason would go down in history as a first-round flop in a draft loaded with future Hall of Famers like John Elway, Jim Kelly, and Dan Marino.

A decade after drafting Eason, the Patriots took Bledsoe out of Washington State with the first pick, and for a while he proved worthy of the billing. Bledsoe put up some huge numbers, and the Pats became a consistent playoff contender.

But then Bill Belichick showed up, Brady got his chance, and history turned on a dime.

Viewed as a line graph, the annals of Patriots quarterbacking are hard to figure: the dips come where there should be spikes, and vice versa. And with Brady, the line has burst off the page.

PLUNKETT

Plunkett would be considered a dinosaur today, a big, lumbering statue who could throw the ball 40 yards on a line but couldn't get out of trouble. It was a style that one day made Plunkett a champion, but in New England it nearly got him killed.

"He was six foot four, 225 pounds when most guys were 6-1, 180," said receiver Randy Vataha. "He really was one of the first modern guys to just stand in there. And he took a beating for it. He got destroyed."

The Pats' offensive line was horrendous for much of Plunkett's early career, and when Chuck Fairbanks arrived in 1973, he installed a college-style offense that exposed Plunkett to more punishment. When the line finally began to jell in 1975 behind John Hannah, it was too late. Plunkett's confidence was shot.

Some of Plunkett's statistics were so bad they were hard to fathom. Take 1972, for instance: 47.6 completion percentage, eight touchdowns, 25 interceptions, 39 sacks, 46.1 quarterback rating. The Pats won three games that year.

"In 1972 my confidence ran into a stone wall," said Plunkett. "I'd never been in a losing situation before."

Plunkett was sacked an astounding 155 times in five seasons with the Pats, a beating that Plunkett still doesn't like recalling.

"I don't want to remember those years," said Plunkett. "Nobody struggled more. It was tough going for me for a while."

The fans in New England didn't help, and the fact that Plunkett was a low-key, west coast guy made it a bad mix. But people who thought Plunkett failed because he was miscast in New England had it wrong. After all, Brady is from the Bay Area just like Plunkett, and he doesn't appear to be having too many problems.

"Jim wasn't miscast out east, he was miscast behind an offensive line that couldn't block. Period, story over," said Pat Sullivan. "Jim Plunkett would have fit in anywhere. Being 'miscast' would apply to Eason more than Plunkett. You could have put Plunkett in the middle of New York or New Jersey and given him the right offensive line and he would have brought the team to the Super Bowl. We just didn't protect him. We did a horrible job at that."

Added Upton Bell: "Plunkett was a great player, but I think the whole situation around the team depressed him. There was always turmoil. By the time [Chuck] Fairbanks got here—it was too late mentally for him."

Plunkett's revival would come years later, but first he endured another failure in San Francisco. The 49ers had sent the Pats a huge package of draft picks (three first-rounders and a second) and the fans were expecting great things from their hometown hero. That stint lasted two seasons. Plunkett was then out of football for a year. Finally, he resurfaced on Al Davis's Raiders, where the long-ball offense happened to suit his pocket style perfectly. It was there that Plunkett fulfilled his Super Bowl destiny, 10 years and 3,000 miles removed from his first day in New England.

THE WARRIOR

How many injuries did Grogan suffer during his career?

How much time to do you have?

"I had five knee surgeries, but none of them were really major except for the one time they had to put two screws in there because I had a broken bone," he began. "The others were cartilage and bone chips. I broke my fibula. I cracked ribs on several occasions. I had a couple of separated shoulders. The biggest surgery I had was when they replaced a disk in my neck. I broke a couple of fingers. I broke my hand once. I stretched ligaments in my knee several times, which didn't require surgery. I had elbow surgery once after I tore a piece of tendon of my throwing elbow. And, of course, I had several concussions. On four or five occasions, I don't really remember what went on for a while. Today, they hold you out for a couple of weeks. Back then if you told them how many fingers they were holding up you went back onto the field."

Grogan went back onto the field plenty during his 16 years, and his toughness came to define his career in New England. The enduring image for most fans is the sight of the gimpy-kneed Grogan lumbering onto the field wearing a bulky neck brace usually reserved for linebackers. The look made sense, because Grogan played like a linebacker. If fans had trouble relating to Plunkett, then Grogan was right up their ally.

That's not to say the love affair was immediate or consistent. Early on, Grogan's temperamental nature got the better of him. He was also prone to throwing the big interception. And fans seem to forget that for every comeback he made through his career, there was a painful benching that preceded it.

"I was popular early on. Then fans hated my guts and then I was popular again," said Grogan. "It was kind of a strange situation. I appreciate the fact that people liked what I did, and I hear people talk about me being one of the toughest quarterbacks to ever play. But I wish they'd say I was pretty good, too."

The record will show that Grogan did a lot more than take a beating. He remains the franchise's all-time leader in passing yards (26,866) and touchdown passes (182). He is third all time in career rushing touchdowns (35). Opponents feared him for his double-threat ability, coaches valued him for his intelligence, and teammates admired him for his leadership.

In 1974, the Pats had Grogan rated as the No. 1 quarterback in the nation, and when he dropped off many draft boards the next year because of a neck injury, Fairbanks was elated. The wily coach then stole Grogan in the fifth round in 1975.

"I took the chance because I knew we had Plunkett to hold the fort while Steve rested his neck," said Fairbanks. "But when Grogan got here he was the best rookie prospect I ever saw. Jim got hurt and we just had to put Grogan in there. And he ended up producing more in eight games than Steve Bartkowski, the No. 1 pick in Atlanta that year, had produced all season.

"Steve's intelligence was the number-one thing," added Fairbanks. "He had something like a 145 IQ. He also had great quickness. He was strong. Competitive beyond belief. In the beginning he was violatile, a little hot-headed. But as he began to mature it was like having another coach on the field."

Steve Grogan *(Jim Mahoney/Boston Herald)*

Best of all, Grogan's teammates believed in him.

"In the huddle the quarterback is the focal point. Everyone is looking into his eyes and you draw strength from it. Grogan had that eye. He was a great leader," said Hannah. "I remember playing Pittsburgh once and Steve got spit on by [defensive end] Dwight White. Grogs tried to spit back, but he didn't have any slobber, so he just sort of made that motion and sound like he was going to spit at White. So White came at him again and Steve just stood there. Didn't back down one inch. Leon [Gray] and I had to break it up. Grogs wanted to fight Dwight White!

"Make no bones about it. That's the kind of guy he was," added Hannah. "He was the kind of guy you wanted to protect, the kind of guy you wanted to play for."

Added linebacker Andre Tippett: "You just knew when he was in the game that something could happen. Tighten up your shoes. You knew he had that special aura. The guy would be out there with the horse collar around his neck, knee braces on both legs. I remember one time he ran into the end zone and he couldn't straighten his leg because his brace had locked up. He nearly hyperextended his knee. He was just that kind of guy."

Meanwhile, Grogan instilled so much confidence from his coaches that he was the team's play-caller through most of the latter stages of his career—whether he was playing or not. Ron Erhardt first gave him the duty in 1979, and Raymond Berry followed suit during the 1985 Super Bowl run. When Eason came on the field, Grogan kept the play sheet.

"It was just my job," said Grogan. "I think I was pretty good."

That experience made Grogan a natural candidate to become an NFL quarterback coach, and for years, he tried to land a job. He knocked on the door in Foxboro several times, but nothing ever materialized.

"I made a run at it, but doors kept closing in my face. And after a while I just got tired of having the doors closed," said Grogan. "If Raymond Berry was in a position to be hiring coaches I would have gone with him, and if Chuck Fairbanks were still in it I probably would have gone with him. I never say never, but the longer I'm out of the game the less likely it's going to happen. To be honest with you, I've talked to every [head coach] on the Patriots since Parcells and let them know I'd be interested. And nobody has made the offer, so here I am. Which is fine. I've had the time to watch my kids grow up and play ball. You accept the way things come in life and you move on."

Today, Grogan is owner of Grogan-Marciano Sporting Goods in Mansfield, Massachusetts. His store specializes in uniforms for youth leagues, high schools and colleges.

He doesn't sell neck braces.

HE SHOULD BE FITTED FOR A DRESS

Eason always had his critics, whether they were in the media, among the fans or even in his own locker room. Hannah was always the worst, and the passage of time never changed that. Hannah once famously said Eason was so soft he should be "fitted for a dress."

It was an opinion Hannah formed before the quarterback even arrived in Foxboro.

"I remember the first time I ever saw him," said Hannah. "It was the Liberty Bowl against Alabama and Coach Bryant. Keith Jackson was announcing the game and I was watching it with a bunch of friends. The game started and almost immediately Eason would get hit and have to leave game. He'd come back, get hit again and then leave the game again. It happened like 15 times! And Keith Jackson was like, 'What a courageous young man.'

"And I looked at my buddies and said, 'Courageous?' He's the biggest chicken shit I ever saw. You leave the game once, fine. But if you leave the game 'a second time it better be on a stretcher. I said, 'I feel sorry for the team that drafts him.'

"And guess who drafts him? [Pats personal director] Dick Steinberg. And we could have had all those guys that year. Kelly. Marino. But we got Eason. Does that tell you anything about Dick Steinberg?

"[Eason] would have been a great baseball player," added Hannah. "He could have stood there and thrown the ball and no one would have touched him. He had a great arm. But he had no courage. He didn't want to get hit."

As for the "dress" comment, that never stood well with coach Ray Berry.

"John should have had his butt kicked for making a statement like that about a teammate," said Berry. "But that was John Hannah."

EASON VS. GROGAN

Despite Hannah's protests, Eason arrived in New England in 1983 and within two years had taken Grogan's job. At the time, most fans were glad to see the change.

The feeling didn't last. Soon, Eason's frailty became apparent, and that only served to highlight Grogan's toughness and work ethic. Eason had the golden arm, but he couldn't stay on the field. And when Grogan came in, things just seemed to happen. In the locker room, the preference for Grogan was resounding.

"Absolutely," said Steve Nelson. "Tony had some unbelievable games, but he was totally opposite of Steve. Physically he just wasn't strong. And Grogan inspired you. You knew he was going to hang in there and do everything he could to win. I think it's very fair to say he inspired the team more than Tony did."

According to Hannah, even players on the other team had a preference.

"I remember playing the Raiders, and I'll never forget this as long as I live," said Hannah. "Eason got tackled hard and had to leave the game, and [Raiders linebacker] Matt Millen went over to the guy who hit him and screamed, 'You dumb son of a bitch! I told you to hit him

There was always a quarterback controversy whether to play Eason (left) or Grogon. *(Jim Mahoney/Boston Herald)*

and scare him, not knock him out of the game! Now Grogan is coming in!' That's what Millen said on the field."

As far as Grogan is concerned, the treatment of Eason was unfair.

"Tony was a good kid," he said. "We got along very well together. And he had a lot of talent as a quarterback. No question about that. He just didn't like the physical part of the game, and that was fairly obvious. He made a comment to me one time: 'Aren't you worried about how you're going to feel when you're 40?' I knew I wasn't going to feel very good, but that was part of the game. He said when he was 40 he wanted to be able to play tennis and do other things.

"That told me right there that, while he had talent, he didn't have the toughness to play the game. And the people around here got on him pretty good about it. He just didn't have enough intensity for the people around here."

Eason's disastrous performance against Chicago in the Super Bowl (zero for six, three sacks) only confounded matters. Most fans remember Eason cowering beneath the unrelenting Bears pass rush and retreating to the bench in favor of Grogan. Coach Ray Berry felt Eason played well on the first series only to be foiled by some bad luck.

Of course, Hannah was among those players who felt Grogan should have started the game all along.

"Why do you think we averaged only 15 throws a game during that postseason?" said Hannah. "It's because we were trying to hide Eason. Because the minute he dropped back, he was looking for a place to fall. In the Super Bowl I turned to Ray Berry and said, 'Either you get Tony out of the game or I'm leaving. I can't protect him anymore.'"

CHAMPAIGN TONY

Eason picked himself up after the Super Bowl debacle and had his best season as a pro in 1986, throwing for a career-high 3,328 yards and leading the Pats back to the playoffs. The record will also show that Easton stood in the pocket and took plenty of hits in the process, getting sacked 43 times.

But Eason's California attitude just never cut it with the fans. People thought he didn't care. People thought he didn't have courage or guts. Grogan's presence made things worse, and when local hero Doug Flutie showed up in 1988, Eason was getting it from all directions. He couldn't win.

"He got a bad rap," said Berry. "He was very much a clutch, money player. We lost our ability to run the ball in 1986 like we had the year before, and Tony had a hell of a year. People seem to forget that.

"But there was definitely a point there where he got gun-shy," added Berry. "He didn't want to get hit anymore—and that's why I eventually cut him."

Indeed, injuries caught up with Eason quickly, and he started only eight games from 1987-89. Where many of his teammates, most notably Grogan, sacrificed their health to stay on the field, Eason refused to take that chance.

"Tony was a very pragmatic, practical and, in fact, cheap guy," said Pat Sullivan. "He had planned out his career. He was going to make a certain amount of money, he wasn't going to kill himself. And the minute he hit that point, he was done. I'm out of here and I'm going to go play tennis. I'm not going to beat myself up like Steve Grogan. He told me that.

"Champaign" Tony Eason scrambles to avoid one of his many sacks. *(Jim Mahoney/Boston Herald)*

"I'll never forget the year we had to waive him (in 1989). Tony separated his shoulder, which wasn't hard for him to do because we was so thin and frail. Eventually (team doctor) Bert Zarins said he was ready to play and Tony walked into my office and I said, 'We're going to activate you this week.' And he said, 'If you activate me, I'm not going to play.'

"I told him that was a violation of his contract. And he said, 'Then you're going to have to do something about it.' I called (owner) Victor Kiam and said we can't stick Raymond with this problem. So I waived him and all hell broke lose. The media wanted to know how I could waive a guy in the middle of the season and not get anything for him."

Revisionist history alert: Sullivan failed to mention that the Pats had also asked Eason to take an in-season pay cut, and that Eason had refused. Eason was soon claimed by the Jets, although he didn't report to New York until two weeks later, until after the Jets had traveled to play, the Pats back up in Foxboro. Naturally, fans thought Eason was ducking out.

"It's a pretty unique situation they've got going on up there," said Eason. "It's hard to describe tactfully.... It got pretty ugly. You have to understand the situation. The fans up there are pretty rabid Flutie fans, to say the least. They had a guy up there they wanted to see play.... They got what they wanted. I was happy to get out of New England, and they were probably very happy to get me out of there."

Eason was always a private and tactful person during his playing days, and that only multiplied once he became a civilian. His father, Charles, said Eason currently lives in northern California where he's in the "financial business" and is the proud father of young twins.

"He just doesn't care about publicity," said Charles. "He's low-key."

And what about the rough treatment in New England?

"That's the way of the world," said the elder Eason.

THE DECISION

Raise your hand if you were among those who thought the Patriots should have drafted Notre Dame's Rick Mirer over Washington State's Drew Bledsoe with the first overall pick of the 1993 draft.

What? No hands?

Come on, we know you're out there.

The Bledsoe-Mirer debate was all the rage in the spring of 1993, and it extended right up into the office of the Patriots' new coach—Bill Parcells. Mirer was more athletic and mobile. He was considered more of a leader, and he had the Notre Dame pedigree. Bledsoe was bigger, had a better arm and was better suited to a pro-style offense. The decision represented a crossroads in the history of the franchise. Owner James Orthwein was on the verge of selling the team or moving it, and Parcells was one of his selling points. The new quarterback would be the other.

Of course, Parcells settled on Bledsoe. In making his decision, Parcells said one of the factors was "certainty," meaning Bledsoe's play in college more closely resembled what would be asked of him in the NFL. Basically, Bledsoe had made every throw in the book at Washington State, while Mirer was hampered by the option offense at Notre Dame. Bledsoe had averaged 34 pass attempts a game in college, Mirer averaged only 19. The analysis proved to be dead on.

Like Mirer, Bledsoe was a coach's son. He grew up speaking the language of football, and the assumption was that Bledsoe would have all the instincts and football intelligence he needed to excel at the next level.

"It's a real advantage," said Bledsoe prior to the draft. "You learn football the way a normal kid learns language. I've known cover-two, cover-three since I was in the third grade."

It turned out to be an ironic quote, since Bledsoe would be criticized often during his pro career for not being able to read defenses quickly enough to avoid the blitz.

Meanwhile, Mirer won the 1993 rookie of the year award and then went straight downhill. He was out of Seattle by 1996 after failing to lead the Seahawks to a single above-.500 season. Mirer immediately became a journeyman backup. One of his stops was with the New York Jets, where then-coach Parcells tried to bring back some of that old 1993 feeling. It didn't work.

BLEDSOE

Bledsoe was yet another west coast guy, another laid-back, even-tempered quarterback who had to adjust to the expectations and energies out east. He also had to adjust to Parcells. Bledsoe came to New England as The Man, the proverbial big fish in a little pond at Walla Walla, Washington, High School and again at Washington State. Bledsoe was used to dictating his own pace, and he soon found out that wasn't going to fly with Parcells.

"Drew used to be an 8:30, 8:45 a.m. sleepyhead kid," said Parcells during that rookie season. "Now he's in at 7:15, 7:30 every day, the way a young kid who needs to learn the game has to be. I like that."

There were small hints of greatness from Bledsoe throughout his rookie season, but the first true sign came in the final week, when Bledsoe threw for 329 yards and four touchdowns in an overtime upset over Miami at Foxboro Stadium. Then, after an uneven start in 1994, Bledsoe exploded on the scene with his performance in a November

Drew Bledsoe *(New England Patriots)*

game against Minnesota. Trailing 20-0 just before half, Parcells went to the no-huddle and Bledsoe started slinging the ball all over the field. He finished with 45 completions on 70 attempts, both NFL records. His three touchdown passes gave the Pats an eventual 26-20 overtime win.

Bledsoe was soon the focal point of the offense, throwing for 4,555 yards on the season. His 691 attempts set another NFL record. At 22, he became the youngest player ever to be selected to the Pro Bowl. And the win over the Vikings propelled the Pats on a seven-game winning streak to close out the season. For the first time since 1986, they were in the playoffs.

The Pats were winners again, but in a way the coach was unaccustomed to. Parcells was used to controlling games by running the ball and playing defense. Suddenly, it was Air Tuna.

"It's not really what we'd like to do," admitted Parcells. "We're always under the gun. We're never in complete control."

Parcells also didn't like how the fans and media, after just two seasons, had put Bledsoe in the upper tier of NFL quarterbacks along with Brett Favre, Dan Marino and Steve Young. Parcells knew it was too early for that.

"He's on the way up. But people are putting him farther up than they should," said Parcells. "We have a tendency to make the ascension process much quicker than it should be, equaled only by the rate of acceleration of the decline."

Again, Parcells was prophetic—although not immediately. Bledsoe separated his shoulder early in 1995, dooming that season. But Bledsoe was back in 1996 to lead a balanced Patriots offense to the Super Bowl. Even though the Pats lost to the Packers, the future seemed bright. Bledsoe was only 24 at the time.

Then Pete Carroll arrived and Bledsoe wound up suffering the same fate as his team. He never went to the next level. There always seemed to be one big play or one big game that eluded him. In 1997, he threw a hideous interception to Pittsburgh defensive lineman Kevin Henry in a late-season loss to the Steelers, which forced the Pats to travel to Pittsburgh in the divisional round of the playoffs. That game ended in hair-pulling frustration as Bledsoe was strip-sacked on the final possession by future teammate Mike Vrabel, and the injury-riddled Pats fell to the Steelers 7-6.

Bledsoe earned redemption the next season, playing through a painful broken index finger on his throwing hand and leading the Pats to dramatic last-minute wins over Miami and Buffalo. The finger couldn't hold up and Bledsoe was in street clothes for the Pats' first-round playoff loss in Jacksonville, but he had still proved a point: He was tough, clutch, and could lead the team without the Tuna. The performance silenced his doubters among the fans and media.

"He was so ripped off when I got there," recalled Carroll. "People thought he was everything he wasn't. He turned out being the captain of that team. A terrific leader in the organization. And when I walked in there he wasn't that. He was everybody's whipping boy. He wound up being the hero. I loved that process. It was one of my favorite things about being there."

Bledsoe came out firing again in 1999 with 13 touchdowns and just four interceptions over the first half of the season. The eighth game was in Arizona, where Bledsoe was splendid in throwing four touchdowns in a 27-3 rout. The only problem was that tight end Ben Coates, who had been Bledsoe's favorite target in the early days but had begun to slow considerably, didn't have a single reception. Coates proceeded to voice his complaints to the media, and when the Pats returned from the bye two weeks later, they weren't the same team. Bledsoe's huge first-half numbers reversed themselves in the second half (six touchdowns, 17 interceptions), and the Pats went from 6-2 to 8-8 and missed the playoffs. Carroll was fired, Belichick was hired, and things have never been the same for Bledsoe or the Patriots.

"He had a bad finish to that third season, and that was a terrible tragedy," said Carroll. "At the break point we were flying. That was when Ben Coates put on that big bitch session, and we never were the same. Drew and Ben were so well-connected. I don't know how it could have been like that, but that's what happened. We lost that connection, and Drew wasn't as effective."

Through it all, from the day he arrived until the day he left, Bledsoe remained the ultimate class act. He had a strong sense of family and a perspective on life that was different from most of his peers. He never said the wrong thing and rarely did the wrong thing. His most quotable moment came after he lost his job to Brady in 2001 when he responded to reporters' queries by snapping, "Next question." Bledsoe's character was his lasting legacy in New England, and it earned him strong allies in the organization, among media members, and with the fans. Robert Kraft once said he considered Bledsoe like a son and that he deserved to be considered alongside Ted Williams, Bobby Orr, and Larry Bird as one of the greatest Boston sports athletes of all time.

But in the end, there was something missing from Bledsoe's football approach. The same deficiencies he had as a rookie—reading defenses, getting rid of the ball on time, moving in the pocket—stayed with him his whole career. Bledsoe had some huge games and some great seasons, but he never seemed to improve.

The fans who felt Bledsoe wasn't tough enough, or didn't want it bad enough, had it wrong. Bledsoe played hurt and he played hard and he never shied away from contact. And, without question, he wanted to win.

The only difference was that Tom Brady wanted to be Joe Montana.

"[Brady] is unique in that regard," admitted Carroll. "They're different people, you know. You can't expect everyone to be like the people you want them to be. Drew is what he is. He battles, he cares a lot. He'll fight you. Some guys just go way beyond that. They're special characters. And, obviously, Brady is a phenomenal character kid. Drew did what he could with what he had, and he continues to do that."

Bledsoe was eventually traded to Buffalo, where Belichick continued to get the better of him and the local fans grew uneasy with their new franchise quarterback after just one season. But the respect for Bledsoe never wavered.

"He's a great man," said Vrabel. "He puts his family first. He did things the right way when he was here. And I don't really expect him to ever do anything different."

10

THE "BS" PATRIOTS, PART II

The Patriots' first Great Era of Utter Ineptitude and Embarrassing Mismanagement occurred from 1969-72. Exactly two decades later, the Patriots suffered another Great Era (1989-92).

In hindsight, it's hard to tell which was worse.

What was more pathetic, Upton Bell rooting for his team to lose so he could fire his coach in 1971, or Victor Kiam insulting a female reporter who had been harassed by his players in his locker room in 1990? What was more embarrassing, Clive Rush's Black Power defense, or Dick MacPherson's sideline hug-a-thon? Who was the worse coach, Jon Mazur or Rod Rust? You can make a case for all of them.

Both eras featured massive upheaval in the ownership, which filtered down to the front office, the sidelines and the field. Neither team won more than six games in a season, and both were rescued by larger-than-life, take-control coaches. It's only fitting that Chuck Fairbanks and Bill Parcells are close friends.

Ultimately, the difference was that the first era just led to more fits and starts by the Sullivans. The second led to the arrival of Robert Kraft.

RUST/MACPHERSON

The two coaches who followed Berry could not have been more opposite in temperament.

Rod Rust was a cold fish with no discernable personality. Could he coach? Probably not, but who really knows? The 1990 season was an utter disaster soon after it started, with the sexual harassment episode involving reporter Lisa Olson breaking in September. By October, federal investigators were crawling all over Foxboro, and everything fell apart. The Pats won once all year.

When Rust convened practice one day in October, he was without five offensive starters, all of whom were gone on non-football business. Tackle Bruce Armstrong and running backs John Stephens and Robert Perryman were meeting with special investigators working the Olson case. Receiver Hart Lee Dykes was in the hospital recovering from wounds to his head and face suffered in a nightclub brawl. And star receiver Irving Fryar was being released from jail after being arrested on a weapons charge the same night.

"You could have put Knute Rockne in there and it wouldn't have mattered," said Pat Sullivan.

Maybe, maybe not. You'd like to think that Rockne would have done better than 1-15. But, then again, maybe the Patriots were beyond salvation.

What followed next was something the NFL had rarely seen before and certainly hasn't seen since. Even by college standards, Dick MacPherson was a rah-rah type. By NFL standards, he was over the top. With MacPherson, it was hugs for everyone. In his first home game as coach, a 24-20 win over Houston, MacPherson tackled quarterback Hugh Millen so hard after a touchdown pass he suffered a busted lip.

MacPherson, a native of Maine and a successful coach at Syracuse, immediately became one of the most beloved people ever to work for the Patriots organization. He got along with players, coaches and media. He looked people in the eye and told the truth. It was impossible to say a bad thing about the guy.

Again, could he coach? Again, who knows? He was handed an awful team, and in 1991 he coaxed six wins out of it. That was pretty good. But MacPherson was another Patriots coach who had absolutely no control over his roster, and even though he was never anything but upbeat and positive on the outside, the job tore MacPherson's guts apart on the inside. Literally. MacPherson missed several weeks in 1992 when he was hospitalized with acute diverticulitis, a stomach disorder brought on by stress. The Pats limped to 2-14 with longtime assistant coach Dante Scarnecchia filling in when MacPherson was in the hospital.

"What a great guy Coach Mac was," said linebacker Andre Tippett. "You just never saw the guy have a bad day. So rah-rah. But in the pros, it's just a little bit tougher to be that way. You've got guys who are getting paid for a living. We weren't on scholarship. Some of the guys were a little taken back by it. I mean, it's just a matter of taking care of business. But we were also in the middle of turmoil. Ownership was changing. It was like, let's put a band aid on it. But I really enjoyed being around Coach Mac."

THE SALESMAN

If Ron Meyer was the biggest fraud to ever coach the Patriots, then Victor Kiam was the biggest fraud to ever own them.

Kiam rose to fame as the owner of Remington shavers, a product he liked so much he "bought the company." Was that also why he spent $84 million on the Patriots? Hard to tell. He wasn't really from New England (Connecticut) and his favorite sport was tennis. He seemed more interested in publicity than pigskin.

"I remember when the deal finally got done, Victor and I were coming back from the league meetings in Dallas and he got on the phone with his wife," said Pat Sullivan, who remained GM through most of Kiam's tenure. "He was obviously beaming about the sale, and he said to her, 'Honey, you can tell the size of the boys by the size of their toys.'

"And to my father, the Patriots were definitely not a toy," added Sullivan. "It was a labor of love."

Kiam was a shameless self-promoter, and his best-selling book, *Going For It*, was an autographical guide to becoming rich. Those around the Patriots wondered how he had ever made so much as a dime. He bought the team in such a haste and did such a poor job on due diligence that he failed to realize he was walking into one of the worst leases in the NFL. Kiam had the team, but he didn't have the rights to parking, concession or luxury box revenue. And after a beef with the man who did own those revenue streams, Robert Kraft, Kiam found himself shut out of his own private suite. He had to watch games from the press box with the unkempt sportswriters, who, he soon realized, had yet to discover his shaving products.

Kiam once famously said: "Money's only important because it's like tennis. You don't earn it to have it, but to read the financial score at the end of the financial year. You do it to win."

Victor Kiam's tenure as owner of the Patriots was highly controversial and never successful. *(Jim Mahoney/Boston Herald)*

Again, those in New England wondered about Kiam's fascination with keeping score. The Pats went 21-43 during his four years of ownership.

"Victor was not a bad person. He probably meant well. But I think his priorities were screwed up," said Berry. "You shouldn't own a football team for the spotlight. I didn't believe in doing things to make a show. If you're going to own a team, your No. 1 priority should be to be the best in the business. I think Victor had other motives. I don't think he really knew what he was doing. But some people buy teams just to step into the spotlight, right?"

LISA OLSON

The definitive example of Kiam's ineptitude came during the Lisa Olson affair, when the supposedly media-savvy owner proved himself to be a chauvinist and a fool on a national stage.

On Monday, September 17, 1990, a day after the Pats had returned from a win in Indianapolis to even their record at 1-1, Olson, a writer for the *Boston Herald*, was attempting to interview cornerback Maurice Hurst in the locker room when several naked players gathered around her and began making lewd comments and gestures. The players named in the incident were Zeke Mowatt, Robert Perryman and Michael Timpson. But an NFL investigation eventually discovered there were even more players involved. Olson never knew how many harassed her because she never gave her assailants the satisfaction of looking up.

All Olson and the *Herald* wanted was an apology from the team and a meeting with the players. Olson didn't want anything to come out publicly. The team delayed. Three days later, the *Boston Globe* published a story on the incident. The *Herald* was forced to follow suit. Then Kiam began opening his mouth and a firestorm ensued.

Four days after the incident, Kiam was overheard calling Olson a "classic bitch" in the visitors' locker room at Cincinnati's Riverfront Stadium. Kiam told the *Herald* the next day that he was misconstrued, then he added: "I can't disagree with the players' actions. Your paper is asking for trouble by sending a female reporter to cover the team."

The Pats conducted their own probe of the incident—which *Sports Illustrated* called "pitiful"—and wound up fining Mowatt $2,000 of his $650,000 salary. Outraged, NFL commissioner Paul Tagliabue finally stepped in and ordered a sweeping investigation to be led by a cadre of former FBI agents.

The Pats promptly disintegrated, as players were constantly pulled out of practices and meetings to testify against other players. The dissension was inevitable. The Pats never won another game.

When Pat Sullivan looked at the bigger picture, he saw conspiracy. Tagliabue was in the process of negotiating a new television deal with the networks, and Rupert Murdoch and FOX were suddenly big players. Murdoch also owned the *Herald*, which was demanding satisfaction on the Olson case. It wasn't hard to put two and two together.

"It was absolutely ridiculous," said Sullivan. "They kept trying to get player 'x' to rat on player 'y' and it just tore the team apart. They did it to everyone in the organization. Coaches. Secretaries. It was an incredible exercise in sacrificing a football team to build this relationship with Murdoch. It cost a lot of people their jobs—including me."

Indeed, Rust and Sullivan were sacked after the season. Sullivan said that Olson later contradicted her story under oath in depositions for her lawsuit against the team. True or not, Olson was completely exonerated by Tagliabue's investigation, and she eventually received a settlement from the team reported to be worth $250,000.

Meanwhile, Kiam never seemed to get it. In February of 1991, while serving as a featured speaker at a banquet in Connecticut, Kiam attempted a hideous joke about Olson and "Patriot missiles." Women's groups were outraged and his shaver business, which catered largely to women, plummeted. He passed away in 2001 at the age of 74.

Pat Sullivan reserved most of his bitterness for Tagliabue.

"It was a pretty sorry deal," said Sullivan. "Tagliabue has been great for the league, obviously, but I have no respect for the guy at all. He had no problem sacrificing certain people to get what he wanted."

THE SPORTSWRITER

Today, Lisa Olson is back in NFL stadiums. She's a columnist for the *New York Daily News* and has covered the Patriots as they've become a national story. She went back inside the cramped home locker room at old Foxboro Stadium in 2001 and has since made several trips inside the new, spacious quarters at Gillette Stadium. What happened the fall of 1990 doesn't even come up. Hardly anyone even remembers.

And that's a good thing. There are far more female reporters in the locker room now than there were in 1990, although Olson, contrary to popular opinion, was hardly the only one back then. NFL teams have gotten smarter, and the Kraft family, in particular, has demanded that their roster be stocked with players of acceptable character. The result, said Olson, is an entirely different atmosphere.

"It's just so comforting to cover the Patriots now," said Olson. "And it's wonderful to see how their organization has completely changed. And not just because of what happened with me, although that was certainly part of it. It's just a really positive thing for me to see that if people do something wrong, they can reverse their fortunes.

"It's one of my favorite organizations to cover now."

That's about all Olson will say about her situation. She doesn't grant interviews about the past and, especially, about the events of 1990. Understandably, she doesn't want to go down in history as "that girl in the locker room." The Lifetime Network wanted to do a feature on her and she said no. Graduate students still call wanting to do their thesis papers on her and she politely declines.

Thankfully, the harassment from "fans" ended a long time ago. In the weeks and months following the incident, Olson received a non-stop barrage of threatening phone calls and letters. The words "Classic Bitch" were spray-painted on the front of her apartment house. The words "Lisa is a slut" were spray-painted on a mailbox in front of the Boston Garden. She returned home to her apartment one night to find the message "Leave Boston or die" scrawled in red on her walls. At a September 30 home game against the Jets, fans chanted her name and bounced an inflated blow-up doll in front of the press box.

Olson was forced to leave the Patriots' beat within a month of the incident. She tried the Celtics beat, but her courtside seat was too exposed. Fans heckled and jostled her. One poured a beer on her. She moved on to the Bruins, but she was spat on by fans in the upper deck. She moved to a press box on a higher level, but was spat on by fans in the luxury boxes. She started wearing hats to games. She was sucker-punched by a fan in Chicago.

It wasn't long before Olson realized she had to get out. So she transferred to a paper in a location as from Boston as she could get—Sydney, Australia.

She was back stateside in a few years, and the calendar has taken care of the rest. There are no more insults, no more threatening phone calls. The hats are back in the closet. The athletes she covers today were in grade school and high school when the incident happened, and none of them seem to know the history. The few that do are respectful. Yankees shortstop Derek Jeter once told her he had to write a high school paper on her.

Olson never saw a dime from the settlement. The vast majority of it went to cover legal fees and travel costs flying to and from Australia to give depositions. With the rest of the money, Olson set up a scholarship fund for young journalism students.

The NFL and other pro leagues have learned from the incident. They now hold orientations and workshops with players on how to treat reporters, particularly women. When the NFL advises teams, they use the Olson case as a "how not to" example. Locker rooms still aren't 100 percent safe for women, but they are infinitely better than they were in 1990.

"The fact is a lot of good has come of it," said Olson. "That's the bottom line."

IRVING

He was the Human Headline.

Bar fights. Car crashes. Cocaine binges. Gun charges. You name it, Irving Fryar did it.

"I'd go to bed, and like any coach, the first thing I'd think was, 'I hope my quarterback is safe and sound,'" said Ray Berry. "And the next thing would always be: 'Okay, where's Irving?'"

When the Pats made Fryar the first overall pick of the 1984 draft, they were counting on the best pure athlete in the draft to bring excitement to Foxboro and put people in the seats. It wasn't an unrealistic expectation. Fryar was that good.

The problem was off the field, where the receiver had a long rap sheet in college featuring drugs and domestic violence. And it wasn't exactly like those incidents were in the distant past. A former girlfriend said Fryar got high on cocaine the night before the 1984 Orange Bowl, which the Cornhuskers lost by a point to Miami, losing the national championship. A book by current CBS sideline reporter Armen Keteyian later charged that Fryar deliberately dropped a pass during the game in an attempt to throw it.

Fryar arrived in New England and things got no better. Prior to the 1985 AFC Championship game in Miami, Fryar's wife, Jacqui, cut him in the hand with a kitchen knife during an argument. Roland James took Fryar's place and fumbled a punt that led to a Dolphins touchdown. After the Super Bowl, Fryar was one of the players named in the team's drug scandal.

In 1986, Fryar had to leave a game against Buffalo with an injury, but instead of going for treatment, he got in his car and sped away from Sullivan Stadium. Minutes later, he wrapped his Mercedes around a tree. Police arrived and were puzzled to find Fryar dangling across the front seat of the car. Wasn't he supposed to be at the game?

"He got into an argument with a tree and lost," explained Berry.

In 1987, Fryar claimed he was robbed at gunpoint outside a Boston jewelry store. The next year, he was pulled over in New Jersey, where police found a suspended license and a rifle loaded with hollow-point bullets. In 1990, Fryar and fellow receiver Hart Lee Dykes went to a club in Providence and got into a heated argument with a group of patrons. The fight went outside, where one man began beating on Dykes with a pair of crutches. Fryar went to his car, got his gun, came back and was hit over the head with a baseball bat.

Fryar called that era in his life, "the mess" and later admitted that "I was filled with drugs, filled with lies, filled with alcohol."

The irony was that Fryar was actually a hard worker and an excellent teammate. His conditioning was always top notch. He was a dedicated blocker. He never complained about not getting the ball.

"From the very first day he got here until the day he left, it was always the same: Unbelievable work ethic," said Tippett. "You would have thought with his background and some of the problems he had that he wouldn't do it the right way, but the guy came to work. He had a blue-collar, lunch-pail mentality. The way he practiced, the way he played. He was a receiver who blocked like a fullback. I looked at him like a little brother—someone you had to keep an eye on. But what a talent."

The organization felt the same way.

"Irving was a very difficult guy to be mad at," said Berry. "He really laid it all out there when he played. He blocked like crazy. And he was completely ego-less. If he had only one ball thrown to him it was never, 'Me, me, me.' We just never got him the ball enough, and that was one of my regrets. We had so much talent and I just couldn't utilize it, and Irving was the best example of that."

Fryar finally cleaned up his act in the early '90s after a religious awakening during a church service, but by that time it was too late to salvage his career in New England. Bill Parcells arrived and Fryar was traded to Miami. After making the Pro Bowl just once in nine years with the Pats (as a kick returner), Fryar went to the Dolphins and made the Pro Bowl in each of his first two seasons as a receiver. Finding God was part of the reason. The other part wasn't hard to figure out, either.

Irving Fryar (80) *(Jim Mahoney/Boston Herald)*

In New England, Fryar had nine quarterbacks in nine years, including the forgettable likes of Tom Hodson, Tom Ramsey, Jeff Carlson, Hugh Millen and Marc Wilson. "It wasn't any use," said Fryar. "The ball just wasn't going to get there."

In Miami, Fryar had Dan Marino. Enough said.

Fryar ultimately moved from Miami to Philadelphia and had three more outstanding seasons as a receiver. Today, he's a minister. He and Jacqui are still together.

"I once worked out an equation that I spent 90 percent of my time on 10 percent of my roster," said Berry. "I shudder to think of how much time I spent on Irving Fryar. It was an on-going project, and I have to say that I feel pretty good about how it turned out."

TIP

If anyone can tell you how far the Patriots have come from the abyss of 1989-92, it's Andre Tippett. The five-time Pro Bowl linebacker joined the Pats in their 1980s comeback under Berry and then was forced to suffer through the hideous decline. He played before crowds at Sullivan Stadium that were lucky to reach 20,000. The players today can't believe the Patriots were once the most irrelevant team in town, but Tippett lived it.

It's too bad, because had Tippett played elsewhere, he surely would have received the national recognition his play deserved. Instead, his brilliance was known only to the Foxboro diehards. Either way, Tippett will go down as one of the best defensive players in team history. He is the team's all-time sack leader (100). He owns the three top single-season sack marks, including an 18.5-sack campaign in 1984. The Giants' Lawrence Taylor was known as the preeminent outside linebacker of his generation, but those who saw Tippett play on a regular basis believe he was in the same tier. When Berry was asked if Tippett could be considered a poor man's Taylor, he snapped, "I don't know what you mean by 'poor man's.' He was every bit as good."

"I think at the time I didn't get the same exposure as some of my counterparts around the league got," said Tippett. "I sometimes look at my trophy case and see all the stuff. Linebacker of the year. Defensive player of the year. Pro Bowls. If that's what you use to measure, then I guess you'd say that I did okay."

In 1990, it was safe to say that Tippett was surrounded by the worst team (1-15), the worst coach (Rod Rust), the worst owner (Kiam) and the worst stadium (Foxboro) in the league. Today, the two-time Super Bowl champion Patriots are considered the model organization in the NFL. They have the best coach (Bill Belichick) and best owner (Robert Kraft) in the league. And their stadium (Gillette) isn't too shabby, either.

"I've thought about this a lot—how we're just the total opposite of what we were back in the day," said Tippett. "But it wasn't really until after I was done playing, when all the information started to come in, that I realized how bad we really had it. At the time, we were just playing football. Sure, we had guys who wanted to go to San Francisco, like me, or the Giants, or other places where they were doing it first class. And we knew things were different here—guys fighting to get an extra pair of socks on game day and things like that. But, in the big picture, I just didn't let it affect me."

Andre Tippett (56) *(Jim Mahoney/Boston Herald)*

And it obviously never soured Tippett on the organization or the area as a whole, because Tippett joined the Pats' scouting department after retirement in 1993 and has been a member of the front office ever since. Today, he's the Patriots' football development and promotions director.

And just as religion played a vital role in Fryar's story, so, too, does it deserve mention in Tippett's tale. That's because Tippett is not your average patron at the Temple Beth Shalom in Needham, Massachusetts, where there just aren't too many six-foot-three, 240-pound former All-Pro linebackers who also happen to be black belts in karate.

When Tippett married the love of his life, Rhonda, in Las Vegas during the Pats' bye week in 1993, he knew a conversion was in his future. The Jewish faith was important to Rhonda, so it became important to Tippett.

"I grew up Baptist, but I wasn't fire and brimstone," said Tippett, a native of Birmingham, Alabama. "So it was easy for me. Once we decided we were going to get married and raise kids, it was a no-brainer.

"I took all the steps necessary to make it happen," added Tippett. "All the research. I found the rabbi I wanted to study under. We talked about everything. The faith. The holidays. Raising children. I've heard people say what a tough thing the conversion is, but I didn't find it to be that way."

Tippett fulfilled the requirements and took the ceremonial dip into the Mikvah bath. Today, he lives in Sharon, one of the most heavily populated Jewish towns in the country, with Rhonda and their children.

"I didn't look at it any other way than this is for me and my family," said Tippett. "We decided that we wanted religion in the house, and it was decided this is how we would do it. We wanted the kids in Hebrew school, to have their Bar Mitzvahs and those kinds of things. And I just wanted to make sure I understood it and that the kids had my full support. Because, to me, the biggest thing about the religion is the family aspect. I've seen Robert Kraft and his son Johnathan and their family holidays and how they approach it—and it's all about their family."

Tippett said he's felt comfortable in the congregation from Day 1.

"I don't know if anyone thought it was something for the hype," he said. "But people who knew me knew I wasn't trying to get anything out of it. They knew where I was coming from. I haven't had any problems with it. Everyone has been very accepting. It's been cool."

11

THE
KRAFT ERA

t's one of Johnathan Kraft's earliest childhood memories, the time his father came home from work and called him into the next room. It was 1971 and Johnathan was seven years old.

"I remember he opened his briefcase," said Kraft. "And inside were these thick, white, perforated sheets of paper, and they had these crooked little red and blue logos on them. I wasn't really sure what they were. I just thought they looked cool. Well, they were Patriots season tickets. The whole pack. That night my brother Dan and I were in our room, and we could hear my mother yelling at my dad through the walls. 'Why did you buy these? We can't afford it!'

"That's how it began for us."

Johnathan's father, Robert, was a rare breed for Boston in those days: He was a football diehard. And like the rest of his brethren, he was excited to see what was going on in Foxboro, where the Patriots had just moved into their new stadium and Jim Plunkett was the new franchise quarterback. Robert wound up with seats in Sec. 217, near the 10-yard line.

"When my brothers and I were younger we'd have to go to religious school every Sunday morning, and the classes would run into the afternoon," said Johnathan. "My mother, of course, couldn't understand the logic of us missing something so important for a football game, so my father would send us to school with notes in our

Robert Kraft, from Patriots fan to Patriots owner. Behind Kraft and his wife, Myra, the New England Patriots Foundation has become one of the top team-related charities in pro sports. *(Jim Mahoney/Boston Herald)*

pockets excusing us early, and then he'd leave the house at around 11:30, telling our mom he had to pick up some things. He'd come get us and we'd go to the game.

"As we got older we'd bring our friends, and we'd sometimes have more kids than my dad had tickets. So we'd get to the gate and my father would push us all through the turnstiles real quick before the guy taking the tickets knew what was happening. Then we'd get to our seats, those bleachers, and we'd all cram in."

Today, Johnathan Kraft and his brothers have all the room they need. And if their mother needs to find them on Sunday afternoons, she can just call the owners' box at Gillette Stadium. That's if she's not there herself.

And Robert?

He's been upgraded slightly from section 217.

THE PURCHASE

It didn't take long for Robert Kraft's love of the Patriots to turn into a dream inside his head. He wanted to attend Patriots games with his family for the rest of his life, but as something more than a season ticket holder. He wanted to own the team.

Kraft pushed himself toward that goal through the early '80s, as his paper and packaging businesses thrived and his financial status grew. At roughly the same time, Chuck Sullivan sent his family over the financial brink with his 1984 investment in Michael Jackson's Victory Tour. By 1985, all three holdings related to the Patriots were being dangled in the market: the land surrounding the stadium, the stadium itself and, finally, the team.

The process started slowly for Kraft, and he approached it differently than anyone else. The big names like Donald Trump, Fran Murray and Victor Kiam—they all focused on the team. It was, after all, the marquee part of the deal. But Kraft took a different tack. He studied the value of the land. He did his due diligence on the stadium lease. And then he came up with a plan.

"My father said all the way back in 1985 that the way to get the team was to first get the land, then the stadium and then use it as leverage to buy to the team," said Johnathan Kraft. "Everyone else went after the glamour entity, the team itself, but Robert believed the only way to make it work was to have the other two things first. He was absolutely right."

In 1985, Kraft, along with partner Steve Karp, bought an operating lease and an option to buy the land around the Stadium. Then, in 1988, Billy Sullivan sold the Patriots to Victor Kiam for $84 million. Kraft thought about buying the team then, but the timing wasn't quite right. The stadium was still in flux, and Kraft was sticking to his plan. Soon, the stadium was put up for auction by the bankruptcy court.

It was rumored that Kiam had agreed to buy the team after doing just 48 hours of due diligence. True or not, he obviously didn't understand the value of the stadium or the covenants in the lease. During the bankruptcy hearing, the judge ruled that the agreement, which ran through 2001, contained language that would result in treble damages if the Pats broke the lease. That made it almost impossible, monetarily speaking, to move the team unless the owner of the stadium signed off on it. In other words, whoever controlled the stadium, controlled the fate of the Patriots.

In the auction, Kiam bid $19 million.

Kraft offered $25 million and was awarded the stadium.

People wondered why he would do such a thing.

"No one really competed with us for the stadium," said John Kraft. "In fact, no one really understood why we wanted such a run-down old building in the first place. No one realized what it meant."

Kiam figured it out the hard way. He still owned the team, but most of the cash flows came through the stadium, so he saw none of that money. Kiam couldn't even take in parking revenue, because the land was also out of his hands. Furthermore, the Pats' radio rights were owned by WHDH, which also happened to be a Kraft property. Kraft had prepaid for the deal in 1988 in the final days of the Sullivan ownership, so Kiam didn't get any money out of that, either. Talk about a financial mismatch. If the Kiam-Kraft relationship were a prizefight, Kiam would have been laid out inside the first round.

Minority owner Murray eventually put a call on his money, and Kiam couldn't meet the demand. So in early 1992, Kiam was forced to sell to Murray cohort James Orthwein. The St. Louis businessman became involved for one reason and one reason only—to move the team to St. Louis or sell it to friends in the Midwest who would.

Again, that was virtually impossible with the ironclad lease in Kraft's hands. Someone finally seemed to realize that, because Kraft was soon offered $75 million to sell his stadium holding. It would have represented a huge profit, and Kraft could have simply taken his money and walked away. Instead, he turned it down. Orthwein and his lawyers then tried to shut Kraft out of the sales process, denying him access to the team's financial records. Meanwhile, the Pats closed out the 1993 season with five wins and everyone assumed they were gone to St. Louis. The newspapers were filled with obituaries.

Kraft stood firm.

Finally, with his options dwindled, Orthwein gave in and sold to Kraft for a then-record price for an NFL franchise: $172 million.

"It was eight long and frustrating years," said Kraft, referring to time between his purchase of the land and the final sale of the team. "It was like being at a train station. First Murray came through... then [Donald] Trump... then Kiam. But I felt all along that the day would come that I would have my chance."

The Pats were once again saved for New England, and fans responded by snapping up 800 season tickets in the first hour of business the next morning. By the end of the day, an astounding 5,958 orders had been taken, shattering the single-day record of 979, which came the day after Bill Parcells was hired in 1993.

The risk for Kraft was immense, and if he thought he got an earful from his wife after buying season tickets in 1971, he had no idea what awaited him the night the deal was settled in February of 1994.

"This was what I dreamed of as a kid, so I just decided to do it," said Kraft. "Was it nuts at the time? Yes. It was not a prudent decision."

Five years later, Kraft would make an even less prudent decision.

THE HARTFORD PATRIOTS

When the speaker of the state's House of Representatives publicly calls you a "fat-assed millionaire," you tend to get the picture.

Representative Thomas Finneran later claimed he was not referring to Kraft when he made that statement (yeah, right), but the point was still clear. Because of politicians like Finneran and others, getting a new stadium built in Massachusetts would be an uphill battle for Kraft and the Pats.

Today, Kraft talks often of the bumps and bruises he suffered in his early days of ownership, and the stadium fight was certainly one of them.

Initially, all Kraft wanted to do was spend hundreds of millions of his own dollars on a new stadium in South Boston (part of the "Megaplex" project). He asked for no public money, just some help on infrastructure costs. For that, he was vilified as an outsider who tried to impose his will on the good people of Southie. Governor Bill Weld endorsed the plan, but all politics are local, and Kraft obviously didn't get local enough.

Fine. But Kraft still needed a stadium, so he came up with another deal for the existing site in Foxboro. Again, he would privately finance the full cost of the stadium. He already owned the land. All he needed from the state was some help improving the access roads in Foxboro. Again, it seemed reasonable enough. Again, he was rejected by Finneran.

At that point, most owners would have said, "thanks for your time" and moved on to a city clamoring for an NFL franchise. That's what Jim Irsay did with his Baltimore Colts and Art Modell did with his Cleveland Browns—and both reaped huge financial rewards because of it.

"We had tried so hard for so long, but we had come to the realization that we couldn't do anything in Massachusetts," said Kraft. "And after all we'd been through, we believed nothing would ever change that."

But like Billy Sullivan before him, Kraft kept trying to make it work in New England. He looked into New Hampshire. He tried Providence. Then he hit the jackpot, landing a stunning deal with the state of Connecticut for a stadium in Hartford. The state would pay up to $300 million to build the facility. It would put up another $100 in infrastructure. On top of that, the state guaranteed 30 years of sellouts. When it was all said and done, the Pats were guaranteed of having the highest revenue-producing stadium in the NFL for three decades. Lawyers from the league told the Krafts it was the single best stadium deal they had ever seen. The total value came to roughly $1 billion.

Kraft accepted the deal at a press conference in Hartford alongside Connecticut governor John Rowland. As the cameras rolled, Kraft wore an expression that was stressed and uncomfortable. The deal guaranteed huge profits, and Hartford was still technically in the New England region. But it was obvious that the idea of playing 93 miles outside of Boston just didn't sit right with Kraft.

Five months later, Kraft abruptly backed out of the deal, claiming the Hartford plan couldn't be completed in time (meaning by the 2002 season). Johnathan Kraft had the foresight to include a termination clause in the original deal that allowed the Pats to back out with no penalty prior to May 2, 1999. The Pats officially cancelled the Hartford deal on April 30.

Eventually, after pressure from the NFL and Boston-area business leaders, the state of Massachusetts agreed to pay $57 million in infrastructure costs for Foxboro. But that $57 million was only a loan; Kraft still had to pay it back. Kraft then built $325 million Gillette Stadium (originally named CMGI Field) on his own dime. Think about it: Kraft turned down $1 billion in free money in Connecticut to spend close to $400 million of his own money in Foxboro, a swing of $1.4 billion.

There haven't been too many owners in the history of professional sports who have turned down deals like that. But in the end, Kraft simply couldn't stand to be the person who moved the Patriots out of Massachusetts.

"It was a long journey that ended up back where we began," said Robert Kraft. "That was a record-breaking deal [in Hartford]. ...But it was never about money. And people who think that don't really understand us. For us, your legacy is what you do for your family and your community."

Of course, Rowland cried bloody murder, claiming Kraft merely used the Hartford deal as leverage to get Massachusetts to fork over the infrastructure money. Kraft flatly denied the charge, but the NFL ultimately paid Connecticut $2.4 million to avoid any future lawsuits.

THE TUNA

When did Patriots football truly "arrive" in New England?

Modern historians put the date at January 21, 1993, when Bill Parcells accepted James Orthwein's offer to take over as head coach. The Patriots have never been the same since.

Thank God.

Like Chuck Fairbanks exactly 20 years before, Parcells arrived in Foxboro and changed everything. Discipline and order were re-established and the weak links on the roster were flushed out. The drafting improved immediately. Perceptions were changed, both internally and around the league. Parcells came to Foxboro with two Super Bowl rings from his days with the Giants, and that success slowly but surely rubbed off on the Patriots.

After winning just 14 games over the previous four years, the Pats qualified for the playoffs in Parcells's second season and advanced to the Super Bowl in his fourth. His four-year record was a middle-of-the-road 32-32, but his significance went well beyond the wins and losses.

With Parcells, the Pats were suddenly legitimate.

Parcells was a larger-than-life character who intimidated his players and mesmerized the fans and media. His press conferences were brilliant, and for the first time anyone could remember, people found themselves tuning in to listen to a coach. He was known as "The Tuna," a nickname he inherited as a linebacker coach on Ron Erhardt's Patriots staff in 1980. Parcells claimed he earned the moniker when his fellow assistant coaches tried to dupe him in the annual Thanksgiving "turkey giveaway" ruse, and he responded by saying, "Who do you think I am? Charlie the Tuna?" Linebacker Steve Nelson told a different story. He said the players called him the Tuna simply because he looked like one. Either way, it stuck.

Parcells is known as one of the greatest motivators ever to walk an NFL sideline, and that skill was in full force in New England. He challenged, cajoled, and wisecracked. Above all, he intimidated. And he never let up until his players were performing at the limits of their ability.

"Parcells was all about scaring the crap out of you," summed up kicker Adam Vinatieri.

Backup quarterback Scott Zolak described a typical Parcells tactic:

"All of a sudden in the middle of a practice he'd walk off, get into his car and drive away," he said. "Just like that. That's when you knew you were in trouble. The next day you'd be in the middle of practice, and from 80 yards away you'd hear this whistle—and there he was. 'Do it again!' he'd scream. And we'd be like, 'You mean back in the huddle?' And he'd say, 'No, stretching!' And we'd have to start the whole practice over. That happened four or five times."

Added linebacker Andre Tippett, whose final NFL season was Parcells's first with the Pats: "Bill just came in and said this is what I want and this is what I expect from you. He didn't lie to you about what the expectations were. He showed no favoritism to anybody. He was tough. Just when you thought practice was over, he'd keep you out there another 45 minutes. He was just trying to establish Bill Parcells's way of doing things."

Parcells was famous for deflecting attention and/or criticism away from his players. Public relations assistants recall walking with Parcells to his press conferences and being asked what the hot story of the day was. When told it was a key fumble by player 'x' the day before, Parcells would respond with a wink and two words: "Watch this." Parcells would then sit behind the microphone and regale the press corps with stories about cruising girls on the Jersey Shore. Or he'd change the subject to something like horse racing. Or maybe he'd just say something so funny or so biting that it had to be written or broadcast. Suddenly, player 'x' was an afterthought.

Face to face, Parcells could be ruthless. He once told Zolak in front of a group of players during practice that they had to renegotiate his contract because he was making too much money. Oddly, Zolak appreciated the honesty. So did his teammates.

"We played a lot of cover-2, and he was always worried about me covering the tight end down the middle of the field," said linebacker Ted Johnson. "Well, he liked to sit in his secretary's office and watch guys come into the stadium in the morning. Sometimes he'd say something to you, and sometimes he'd just look at you a certain way. If you were lucky, he let you pass without anything. But one day, he stopped me. This was my second year, my first year calling the defense. He was like, 'Johnson, are you going to be able to cover that tight end down the middle?' I had really screwed it up the day before. But I said, 'Coach, I got it. I swear. Trust me.' And he said, 'I know you'll get it, but when? Is that why in college your best games were the bowl games? Because you had a month to prepare for them? If you had two weeks to prepare for every game you'd be in the Pro Bowl by now.'

"He could rib you pretty bad," added Johnson. "But it was always dead-on. And a lot of guys responded to it, including me."

Players have said that Parcells had a "personal touch" that made the brow-beating just a part of a bigger picture. Parcells got to know the lives of his players. He knew which ones had kids and which had pets. If either were sick, he'd inquire about it. And when players showed up at team functions, he would be on a first-name basis with the wives, whether he had met them or not.

"He was a loudmouth and a bully, but when you got him one on one, it was obvious he cared," said one longtime Pats employee. "He really did a lot of things for people that no one ever knew about. I think a lot of the other stuff was for show."

"Parcells was definitely a psychologist," added Johnson. "He was more concerned about what makes a player tick, and every now and then he'd engage you in a way that wasn't about football. I've always said he made an impersonal business personal."

Parcells had such a hold on the players that when he left for the Jets they still felt his pull. And those who were still around when he returned as coach as the Cowboys in 2003 said the feeling hadn't dissipated.

Bill Parcells *(New England Patriots)*

"It's the strangest phenomenon," said Johnson. "Even if you aren't being coached by him, he has this ability to get you to want to play hard for him. Bottom line, that's what made him a very good coach. You didn't want to disappoint him. I don't think it ever leaves. It's hard to explain."

THE DIVORCE (FAIRBANKS, PART II)

When Robert Kraft bought the Patriots, he automatically assumed he would be able to run it like his other businesses. He figured his top employees would share information and work together on a common goal. He assumed that his people would be committed to the organization and, at the very least, be respectful of those who ran it.

Simple stuff, right?

With Parcells it was never that simple, and Kraft soon discovered that the coach he inherited had his own ideas. Kraft found Parcells wasn't exactly forthcoming with his time during the week or with information about the team. He found that his popular and charismatic coach had no desire to contribute to the public relations efforts that were so vital in the early days of his ownership. Kraft found that while Parcells had a long-term contract, there seemed to be constant uncertainty regarding his future. Parcells liked to evaluate his situation year to year, and Kraft, like most successful businessmen, was in the habit of building for the long term.

It's been said that Bill Parcells is all about Bill Parcells, and if an owner can live with that, then he's a perfect coach. But Kraft had just paid a record sum for an NFL franchise, and he needed more. The Pats were still a long way from being a stable entity. They needed a new stadium. They needed sustained success on the field. They needed a coach who wasn't going to bolt at a moment's notice.

Meanwhile, Parcells was clearly more comfortable with the free rein he had been given under Orthwein. He found Kraft meddlesome to a fault, especially for an owner who was such a neophyte to the NFL. Parcells was a proven success and had been hired to do a job—why couldn't he just do it?

It was a bad match from the start, and the situation probably would have boiled over sooner had the Pats not gone on their seven-game winning streak to close out the '94 season. That year energized the fan base and gave Kraft a playoff appearance in his first season. It made all the little things happening behind the scenes more palatable.

One of those things was Parcells's insistence that director of football operations Patrick Forte be shown the door, a maneuver that allowed Parcells to assume even more control over the football decisions. The key word was "assume," because Parcells was never contractually guaranteed final say on personnel. He had that power for much of his tenure, but only because ownership granted it. It was never a written covenant.

It would prove to be an important point, because in 1995 the Pats dipped badly with Parcells wearing both the coach and GM hats. Their 6-10 finish certainly had something to do with Bledsoe's bad shoulder, but Parcells himself admitted he wasn't at his best in '95.

The scales of power shifted that offseason, as Kraft asserted the authority of head scout Bobby Grier, who had been promoted to director of player personnel the year before. Starting in the '96 off season, Kraft determined that Grier would have the final say.

Kraft was later torched in the media for the decision, but it wasn't without reason. Parcells's record choosing players the previous three years was good but not great. He did well cleaning house early on, but his dips into free agency were mixed, as Giants castoffs Myron Guyton and Reyna Thompson were high-priced busts in the secondary. The drafting, however, was mostly strong, starting with the decision to take Bledsoe over Rick Mirer with the first overall pick in 1993. From there, Chris Slade, Todd Rucci, Vincent Brisby, Troy Brown, Willie McGinest, Max Lane, Ty Law, Ted Johnson, Curtis Martin, Jimmy Hitchcock and Dave Wohlabaugh were all drafted over the next three years to give the Pats a formidable core.

But, again, when Parcells's personnel responsibilities were at their greatest, his coaching performance was at its worst. And soon after the '95 season, Parcells asked Kraft to void the final year of his contract (1997). Kraft readily agreed. That made Parcells, who also had some health issues, a one-year-and-out prospect heading into the '96 season. Not many owners would give a coach total control in that situation—and Kraft didn't.

It all blew up in the draft room in 1996, when Kraft calmly told Parcells that Grier had the control and that the Pats would therefore select Ohio State receiver Terry Glenn with their first-round selection (No. 7 overall). Parcells, who had wanted to trade down to take a defensive lineman, protested but was overruled.

"For about 24 hours, I made up my mind I was finished here," Parcells later told good friend and Boston Globe columnist Will

McDonough. "I didn't want any more to do with this guy [Kraft]. But now here's what I'm going to do. I'm going to get in the greatest shape of my life. I've already started to lose weight. I'm not leaving here 6-10. I'm going to come back here and prove I'm better than that. I did a lousy job [in 1995]. I know that. But next year we've got a chance to be pretty good. I'm just going to have as little to do with this guy as I can and just focus on coaching the team. Then when it's over, I'm out of here. I'm going to retire. This will be my last year coaching."

Parcells's commitment showed, because in '96 the Pats just kept winning despite the off-field rumblings. It helped that Parcells had been reunited with longtime defensive assistant Bill Belichick, who was coming off five disappointing years as head coach in Cleveland. It also helped that the roster was loaded, just like it was in 1978, when the Pats piled up victories despite Fairbanks's impending departure.

It was only fitting, then, that Fairbanks attempted to intercede in the Parcells-Kraft rift. Having experienced it himself, Fairbanks wrote to the two men imploring them to find common ground.

"I tried to tell both of them that they needed each other," said Fairbanks. "That they needed to understand each other's problems. I told Bill he needed to understand the ownership issue, which involved huge, huge dollars. I recommended that they set up regular lines of communication and set aside time to talk things over. But they didn't need me. They had their own thing, and it was hard for them to live with each other, I guess."

Of course, it was Parcells who wound up uttering the most notable words from the dispute. They have now entered the New England sports lexicon.

"If they want you to cook the dinner," said Parcells, "they ought to let you buy the groceries. ...Okay?"

SUPER BOWL XXXI

It turned out Kraft and Parcells had to share the kitchen all the way to the Super Bowl, and the resulting media circus overshadowed everything else that week in New Orleans. Brett Favre and his addiction to painkillers? Drew Bledsoe's ascension to NFL superstardom? The game itself? All of it became page two material.

Most of the good stuff came through leaks. Parcells had plenty of friends in the media, and Kraft at that stage wasn't exactly shy, either. As a result, it was well known that Parcells was out as coach and that his likely destination was the Jets. It also came to light that if Parcells went elsewhere in 1997, the Pats would be entitled to compensation. It was established beyond a doubt that Parcells and Kraft couldn't stand each other.

The week kicked off with Parcells's agent, the late Robert Fraley, leaking word that Parcells would formally quit after the Super Bowl.

Nice way to get your team ready for a big game, no?

"It's unfortunate that his agent, Mr. Fraley, took this time to put something in the paper," said Robert Kraft that Tuesday. "I've waited two-thirds of my life to get here and this game is all I'm going to focus on. I'm not going to let any foolishness or some other people's agenda distract us from one of the great weekends ever in New England."

Meanwhile, Parcells spent much of the week snapping at reporters who brought it up. He may have been a free talker off the record, but when the cameras were on it was a different story.

"My agent didn't talk about it. That's old news," said Parcells during a typical exchange. When one reporter mentioned that it had become "new" news, Parcells shot back: "Next question." When another pointed out that the entire story had to have an effect on the team, Parcells snapped: "I disagree with that statement. I disagree with that statement."

That went on all week. Kraft tried to lighten the atmosphere during one mid-week press conference, but his attempt at humor failed badly. Joining Parcells on the podium, Kraft announced that Parcells had just signed a 10-year contract...to manage one of Kraft's paper businesses. The joke was met with an uncomfortable silence, as reporters looked at each other to see if they had heard correctly. It was so bad that the NFL included the phrase "tongue in cheek" in their printed transcripts, just so unwitting reporters weren't confused.

The Patriots wound up getting beat by the Packers, 35-21. It was clear the better team won, but there were still some coaching decisions made throughout the game that had Pats fans scratching their heads.

Twice, defensive coordinator Al Groh called for safety blitzes, and twice Favre picked them up and threw long touchdown passes. The first came on the Packers' second play from scrimmage with rookie safety Lawyer Milloy covering speedy veteran receiver Andre Rison. It was a mismatch that Favre quickly recognized and exploited.

Then, after the Pats had climbed back into the game in the third quarter on an 18-yard run by Curtis Martin, Adam Vinatieri was allowed to kick off to Green Bay special teams ace Desmond Howard, who had been blazing all playoffs and had racked up two big punt returns in the first half (32 and 34 yards). Instead of a squib kick or a directional kick, Vinatieri's boot was right to Howard, who returned it 99 yards for the decisive score. That gave the Packers a 14-point lead they would not relinquish, as left tackle Max Lane was suddenly left alone against Reggie White and the future Hall of Fame defensive end made the Pats pay with a pair of fourth-quarter sacks. Bledsoe finished the game with four interceptions.

When the dust settled, everyone seemed to ask the same question: Why wasn't Vinatieri told to kick away from Howard?

"It never came up," said Vinatieri.

Apparently, the coaching staff (Mike Sweatman was the special teams coach) had determined that Howard wasn't much of a threat on kickoff returns.

"Howard had had a really good year returning punts. But his kickoff returns weren't that great," said Vinatieri. "In fact, the other guy they had back there [Don Beebe] was actually better that year. Howard's stats were pretty average, and we watched him on film and thought he wasn't that dangerous."

Statistically, Vinatieri was right. Beebe was the Packers' top kick returner in 1996 with a 26.9-yard average and a touchdown return. Howard had a 20.9-yard average with no touchdowns.

Still, the fact was that the Pats' special teams handed the ball to Howard all game, as he was allowed to return five punts for a total of 90 yards. Only one Tom Tupa punt went out of bounds and just one resulted in a fair catch. Even the young Vinatieri had an inkling that sending the ball to Howard at that juncture late in the third quarter wasn't the most prudent course of action.

"But I was a rookie at that point, so it's not like I was going to say anything," said Vinatieri. "If that happened today, I would probably pipe up. But back then it was like, 'Whatever you say, boss.' So we kicked it down to the 1-yard line, he got the opening and brought it all the way back. That's the way it goes sometimes."

What made it worse was that Vinatieri had a chance to tackle Howard before he reached the sidelines. But just as Vinatieri was closing in, he had his jersey held by Packers' rookie linebacker Keith McKenzie. It was a blatant penalty, but the Pats didn't get the call.

"I had a good chance at him," said Vinatieri, who has always been a strong tackler throughout his career. "And if I didn't bring him down, I think I at least would have slowed him enough or made him cut back

The Patriots' second Super Bowl was another loss. *(Jim Mahoney/Boston Herald)*

and someone else would have. It's one of those things I'm still a little upset about. There should have been a flag."

There was another, behind-the-scenes factor involved in the play. In the days leading up to the game, there was an internal debate among the Patriots' coaches over one of the final roster spots. Most of the assistants favored the continued activation of Troy Brown, who had played all 16 regular-season games and both postseason contests. Brown at that point was on his way to becoming a top-notch possession receiver and a special teams stalwart, but in Super Bowl XXXI Parcells ordered that second-year receiver Hason Graham receive the final roster spot over Brown.

How did that work out for Parcells? Not so well. Graham was not only on the field for Howard's decisive return, but it was Graham's lane that Howard breezed through before hitting the open field. No one will ever know if Brown would have clogged up that lane, but he certainly couldn't have done any worse. Graham never played another

NFL game while Brown went on to become a franchise receiver and returner for Pete Carroll and Bill Belichick. Oh, and Brown was never a healthy scratch again.

Nearly to a man, the players on the Patriots said the coaching controversy didn't affect their performance or preparation during the week. They said Parcells and his staff went about their business as usual. One veteran said the only time it seeped into the team setting was after the game, when Parcells's postgame remarks to his players were noticeably flat.

Still, the questions lingered. It was later reported that in the weeks leading up to the Super Bowl, Parcells made over 50 calls to Hampstead, New York, which is the headquarters of the New York Jets. He also must have spent at least a few minutes planning his exit strategy, because he skipped the Pats' team plane the next day, opting to fly separately back to Boston with his agent.

Whether the situation affected the outcome of the game or not is a matter of personal opinion. But it's hard to see how it could have helped, and no one can say that Parcells was at his best that day. Parcells' actions look even worse when compared to the style of Bill Belichick, who has proven to be maniacal in his emphasis on putting nothing or no one ahead of the "team." After the Pats' stunning 2001 Super Bowl season, for instance, Belichick signed a two-year contract extension with Robert Kraft. It was hardly the type of news that would cause a distraction, but even on that Belichick remained firm: He didn't allow the news to be released until a full year later.

Parcells? He couldn't keep his contract situation out of the papers for a week, never mind a year, and that particular week happened to be one of the most important ones in Patriots history. Parcells ultimately got his way, of course, as the Jets agreed to send the Pats four draft picks to bring in the Tuna. Parcells left New England without saying goodbye to his players or the fans.

Kraft did not fare well in the court of public opinion, as the fans blamed him for forcing out the best coach the organization had ever seen. As was the case with his fight for a new stadium, Kraft took his lumps quietly.

Meanwhile, there was an ominous sense of release among the players. "You'd like to think that you go through some things with the guy, at least say goodbye. But that's the way Bill is. From the get-go, Bill is about Bill, and that's the way he is," said Bledsoe. "We've got something to prove as a team. When we went to the Super Bowl, it was turned into a deal where it was Bill Parcells vs. the Packers. And at times, it was like this team was just Bill. So we have something to prove—that it was the players that made the plays that got us where we were."

PETE (RON ERHARDT, PART II)

After four years of intimidation under Parcells, the players were clear in what they wanted in their new coach. They wanted someone who would instill trust and confidence, not fear. They wanted to be "treated like men." They wanted what every team wants after spending years under the thumb of a disciplinarian. Remember the cliché?

They wanted a players' coach.

They got their wish.

Eight days after the Super Bowl and just four days after Parcells officially stepped down, Kraft quickly settled on San Francisco defensive coordinator Pete Carroll as the new coach. Young, upbeat and energetic, Carroll was an immediate departure from the Tuna. He showed up with a big smile and quickly loosened the reins in the locker room.

The players had their freedom, and it didn't take long for them to start enjoying it.

"Guys totally took advantage," said one veteran player. "It was a window that wasn't open when Bill was there. Guys started being late for meetings. Even Pete wouldn't show up on time. Guys were falling asleep in the film room. The sight of Chris Canty with his sunglasses on and his feet up on the desk was all you needed to know. I can't remember how many times Pete would have to stop meetings and say, 'Guys, shush, quiet down!' When Bill was here, everyone was 15 minutes early and you could hear a pin drop. Everyone was on eggshells the entire time he was here."

The new atmosphere wasn't confined to the privacy of the meeting rooms, either. Midway through Carroll's first year, with the Pats barely keeping their heads above water at 6-4, Bledsoe, Zolak, and Lane dove off a stage during a rock concert at a Boston nightclub, injuring at least one young woman. Three days later, the Pats were demolished in Tampa, 27-7, and the "mosh pit" incident came to represent the lack of discipline under Carroll.

Said Vinatieri: "He just wasn't the hard-nosed coach we were used to. He was a great guy, and obviously he was a great coach. Practices were fun. God love him. But Pete tended to always look on the bright side and see the best in people. So somebody would do something wrong and he'd give them another chance. Someone would screw up and it would be like, 'Oh, well. Whatever.' And, in my opinion, that's not what we needed at that point. Sometimes you have to hold people accountable."

It never seemed to improve. Late in Carroll's third and final season, veterans Lawyer Milloy and Vincent Brisby attacked each other with pool cues at a billiards hall during a team charity event. The two renewed acquaintances the next morning, continuing their fight in a meeting room while stunned teammates and coaches looked on.

In hindsight, Carroll had been put in an impossible position—and the players knew it. Not only was Carroll following in the footsteps of one of the most charismatic and commanding personalities in pro football history, but Carroll's ability to control the locker room was severely hampered by Kraft's new organizational structure. Carroll was the coach, but Grier was in charge of the roster and vice president Andy Wasynczuk was in charge of the salaries. That meant Carroll couldn't pick his players and he couldn't pay them, either. What did that leave him? Not much.

It was shades of Ron Erhardt all over again.

Foxboro Stadium had a back stairway that led from the corner of the locker room up to Grier's office. That back route was both literal and figurative, because the players soon realized that Grier's door was always open to their complaints. So even when Carroll did try to crack down, the players merely escaped out the rear hatch.

Carroll attempted some counter measures. Prior to the 1997 playoffs, he opened up the voting for the team captaincy, a move that cost Pro Bowl left tackle and Grier confidant Bruce Armstrong his title. And, in the dying days of 1999, Carroll suspended Glenn for violating a host of team rules. Glenn had always counted on Grier as an ally, and time and again, Grier kept his prize draft pick out of trouble. But, as a final statement, Carroll let everyone know just where he stood on the oft-troubled receiver.

"Any organization that's run with a divided leadership, how can you expect to have a clear message?" said Carroll. "That was obvious to me early, and I couldn't do anything about it. I failed to get that adjusted during the time I was there, but it couldn't be more clear. The adjustment was made with Bill Belichick, and he controls all the things you need to control. And that's all the coaches want in the NFL, but very few of them get it."

Carroll never denied that following Parcells was an uphill battle.

"Bill has a different style than I do," said Carroll. "He coaches differently than I do and differently than most coaches do. He's charismatic and he's one of the great coaches in the history of the game. He ain't an easy act to follow. But we did follow him, and we did win and we did do all right."

Meanwhile, Ray "Sugar Bear" Hamilton, a defensive line coach on Carroll's staff, said the different styles of Parcells and Carroll had nothing to do with the results on the field.

"That was all stupid," said Hamilton. "That was the media and that was perception. When we came there the players were saying they wanted to be treated like men because Parcells had too much of a thumb on them. And then we left and they said they needed more discipline. At some point, the players have to take some damn responsibility."

MARTIN LANDING

Carroll's three years in New England followed a simple, clearly defined pattern. In 1997, the Pats finished 10-6 and were ousted in the second round of the playoffs. In 1998, they went 9-7 and exited in the first round. In 1999, it was 8-8 and out of the playoffs. Carroll remained true to himself to the bitter end, waving and pumping his fists to crowd as he walked off the field following the season finale in 1999. He knew it was his final game, but that didn't stop him. The next day, he took the time to shake the hand of every media member who had covered him the previous three years before jumping in his gold Jaguar and driving out of the Foxboro Stadium parking lot.

During his three years, Carroll was hurt by several factors that had nothing to do with the off-field story lines. The injury bug bit hard, and most every star that Carroll inherited (a list including Willie McGinest, Ted Johnson, Glenn, Martin, and Bledsoe) missed significant time during his tenure. The Pittsburgh playoff loss came with Martin on the sidelines, and the Jacksonville postseason defeat came with Bledsoe in street clothes.

Carroll was also hurt by a talent pool that quickly dried up under Grier. The Pats were awarded four draft picks from the Jets in the Parcells settlement, and Grier used those to select four imminently forgettable players: running back Cedric Shaw, offensive lineman Damon Denson, receiver Tony Simmons and linebacker Andy Katzenmoyer. The 1997 draft was a horror show, with undersized, overmatched cornerback Chris Canty coming in the first round. The poor drafts killed Carroll's depth and made every key injury hurt.

But ask Carroll today why his teams never accomplished more and he'll point to one reason and one reason only. To him, nothing was more important than the loss of Martin to Parcells and the Jets in 1998.

It was a masterstroke by Parcells, who had intimate knowledge of the Pats' salary cap and was able to devise a six-year, $36 million offer sheet for Martin, a restricted free agent, that would have put the Pats in a financial pickle had they matched it. The key to the deal was a clause that gave Martin the option to play for one year at $4 million and then become an unrestricted free agent after the 1998 season. Kraft considered the provision a "poison pill" and petitioned the NFL to nullify the offer sheet. The Pats lost the appeal, although the league decided to forbid such ploys in the future.

The Pats also misjudged Martin's durability, believing the Jets' offer was way too high for a player with a history of knee and groin injuries. It proved to be a bad miscalculation, as Martin would go on to play in 95 of 96 games for the Jets over the next six years. By declining to match the offer sheet, the Pats were awarded the Jets' first- and third-round picks, which Parcells had no problem handing over to Grier. Those picks netted the Pats running back Robert Edwards, who never had a chance to prove himself after a devastating knee injury following his rookie season, and fullback Chris Floyd, who was a bust the day he arrived in Foxboro.

Behind Martin and Parcells, the Jets won the AFC East in 1998 and advanced all the way to the AFC Championship game.

"You can cut it up any way you want, but we won the division in 1997, then we gave Curtis away to the Jets and they won the division," said Carroll. "It couldn't be any more obvious. You can look at a million things, but the best player on the team was given away—to our opponent. It was a shrewd move by Parcells, and he won with it."

And what about the bad drafting by Grier?

"Everybody's drafting is spotty," said Carroll. "Everybody misses on that stuff. That was a factor, but it wasn't the factor. I mean, the Chris Canty draft? That was one of the worst picks ever. He never did a thing. But everyone has skeletons in their closet like that.

"The bottom line is we did all right," added Carroll, who knew his three-year Patriots record off the top of his head. "27-21. That's not bad. A lot of guys would like to have that record. But just think what those last two years would have been like with Curtis. Yeah, we could have coached better, and we could have drafted better, but give us that guy back, and it's a whole new ballgame. It's not that hard to figure out."

EXONERATION

On the night of January 2, 2000, just hours after the Pats defeated the Baltimore Ravens in the season finale at Foxboro Stadium, Carroll and Robert Kraft had a heart-to-heart talk. Carroll told Kraft that if he wanted to turn his team around, he had to give his next coach the power and freedom to make the football decisions. The "committee" approach that existed during Carroll's tenure would never work in the long term. Carroll said Kraft could take it or leave it, but that was his advice.

The discussion must have made an impression, because Kraft wound up giving Bill Belichick all the control he took from Parcells and never gave to Carroll.

For that, said Carroll, the Krafts deserve a huge amount of credit.

"They learned as owners—on the job," said Carroll. "They set up a situation that forced Bill Parcells to leave. He couldn't live with the way it was organized, and he's one of the greatest coaches in the history of the game. Then I followed, and we weren't well structured at all, in my opinion.

"And then they figured it out. You can understand why they didn't know at first. They were new owners. Why should they have all the answers? It's a smart family, but during the time I was there they were still trying to figure out how to run the thing. They went through a couple of coaches in the process, and they finally figured it out. It's a great story, it's just that some people fell off in the process."

Carroll may have been one of those to "fall off," but he has landed quite nicely since. As the head coach of the 2003 co-national champion USC Trojans, Carroll has proven his abilities beyond a doubt.

Could it be that, like Rick Pitino in basketball, Carroll is simply better suited to being a college coach than a pro coach?

"I don't know about that," said Carroll. "I know I'm in charge here. I'm having absolutely the time of my life doing this, and I'm absolutely in charge of the whole thing. Would I have been different in New England if I was in control? It totally would have been different."

Carroll was often ridiculed for his rah-rah style and for saying corny things like "pumped" and "jacked." But the record will show that Carroll had more wins in his three years in New England (27) than either Parcells (21) or Belichick (25) had in their first three seasons at the helm.

"Rah-rah, or emotional, or however you want to look at it—it's just how somebody phrases it," said Carroll. "And you guys [in the media] latch onto that stuff. Because it's comfortable, it's easy and it makes sense. And that's how you do it.

"It goes back to one of the first characterizations of me that was ever put together there. It was a cartoon in the newspaper of me going into my first training camp. It had Bill Parcells on one side and he had these pearl-handled pistols like General Patton. And I'm sitting there on the other side with a surf board and a glass of wine. The Beach Guy....

"And it never changed. You guys stuck on that, and you never even asked the right questions. You didn't know who I was or what I was all about. You never figured it out. I've been allowed to be figured out, because they've let me have my run here. It's a different deal.

"To think that our program in New England was soft, or wasn't aggressive enough.... Jack, I coached defense all those years and I was nothing but demanding and strict and disciplined. Look at my teams right now. We're one of the most disciplined teams in college football. We get penalized the least. We handle the football the best. We don't turn it over. All the things that stand for discipline—not the discipline that you would think of—but the discipline that matters on the football field, that's what we're about. And that's what we were working towards in New England. Just look at our turnover ratios there. They were at the top of the league until Drew started having his problems in the second half of that last year."

True enough. In 1997 and 1998, the Pats set franchise records for fewest fumbles (16 in both years) and fewest total giveaways (22 in '97, and 24 in '98) in a season.

"Those are the things that depict discipline," said Carroll. "It was all about perception. I'm no different now. I don't coach any different now than I did there. Am I better suited to it? I'm better suited to being in charge."

Remarkably, Carroll was also blamed for the injury bug that befell the Patriots during his tenure. It was said that not enough players participated in the off-season workout program, and therefore they weren't physically prepared for a long, 16-game season. It was another charge that Ray Hamilton found ridiculous.

"Pete was a great coach. Pete was fine," said Hamilton. "I think there was always an East coast, West coast thing with him, trying to make him out as soft. Like if someone got hurt, they'd say the weight program wasn't tough enough. Well, what does the weight program have to do with a broken ankle? The same guy gets hurt now and they don't say shit.

"I mean, we made the playoffs two out of three years. I'm not sure what the people up there were expecting. Before Pete got there, they had made the Super Bowl just once with Parcells. Then we got there, made the playoffs twice in three years and everyone was bitching and moaning. They were acting like they had a dynasty—like they were the Yankees or something."

In the final analysis, while Carroll caught the heat for the Pats' decline in those years, he was merely a member of a committee. And that put him in the worst possible position with the players and the fans.

"There were no clear lines on how it was all supposed to be done," he said. "It was, 'work it out.' And it was very difficult. And Robert knows this. It's the conversation we had on the day I walked out.... It's really simple. Robert Kraft doesn't run his business with a bunch of other people making the decisions for him. He does it. When a coach needs a player, he needs to get the player he needs. And if it doesn't work, it doesn't work. But to have someone else chose players for a coach—that's not going to go.

"So when I was having to talk on behalf of other people, that was hard. That was hard representing three different opinions and protecting it all. It would be difficult for anyone. But you have to, because you're a company guy and you have to do the right thing. That's why the press conferences were so hard and it was hard to be clear.

"But I'll tell you what: It ain't hard anymore."

POSTSCRIPT

The 1996 season may have been the end of Robert Kraft's working partnership with Bill Parcells, but it marked the true beginning of his relationship with Bill Belichick.

So as it turns out, '96 happened to be a very good year.

That was the season Parcells promised to have "as little to do with" Kraft as possible, which left the owner with few places to turn for information about his $170 million investment. Enter Belichick, who had no problem extending his owner the common courtesy of answering his questions. Kraft stayed close to Belichick that season, and as the storm clouds gathered with Parcells, Kraft was able to learn about football and the man who would one day run his football organization.

Kraft was impressed with how Belichick worked with the young defensive stars on the team, a list including Lawyer Milloy, Ty Law, Ted Johnson and Willie McGinest. He saw how the Pats' defense, which had been a mess in 1995, was suddenly playing to a championship level. And, most importantly, Kraft discovered that Belichick possessed an intellect he could relate to. Belichick was an economics major at Wesleyan and Kraft was a Harvard MBA. It turns out they spoke the same language.

After Parcells maneuvered his way out of New England following the Super Bowl, Kraft considered naming Belichick as his successor. And eyebrows were raised two days after the Pats returned from New

Orleans when a bomb threat cleared out the offices at Foxboro and Kraft and Belichick climbed into Kraft's car and drove off together. But, in the end, the timing wasn't right. Belichick was still closely linked with Parcells, at least publicly, and the wounds from that season were raw. Kraft was in desperate need of some fresh air, so he went with Carroll.

Three years later, on January 27, 2000, Kraft would once again have Belichick in the front seat of his car. Only this time, they were driving into the Foxboro Stadium parking lot to announce Belichick as Patriots coach. This time, Kraft didn't let Belichick get away.

What happened in between is another saga itself. While the Pats suffered through the Carroll-Grier era, Belichick bade his time under Parcells with the Jets. And when Parcells abruptly retired the night of the 1999 season finale, the assumption was that Belichick would simply take over. In fact, Belichick's contract stipulated that he was required to do so.

Early the next morning, the Patriots sent a fax to Jets headquarters seeking permission to interview Belichick for head coach and GM openings. Permission was denied. Less than 24 hours later, Belichick dropped a bombshell, handing Jets president Steve Gutman a hand-written note that said he was resigning as "HC of the NYJ." Belichick then stepped to the podium in a room packed with reporters—who were there to cover Belichick's introduction as Jets coach—and tried to explain himself during a rambling, 45-minute press conference. It was chaos.

While the decision stunned some observers, those who knew Belichick well found it to be no surprise at all. Belichick had worked for Parcells for 16 years, and by that point he had clearly had enough. Belichick was convinced that if he took the Jets job, Parcells would still be hanging over his shoulder in the front office, controlling the football decisions and making his life miserable. Belichick also knew from experience that Parcells was liable to change his mind at a moment's notice and return to the sidelines.

Parcells later claimed that the Pats tampered with Belichick at some point during 1999, making it clear to Belichick that a coach/GM role awaited him in New England. True or not, the fact is that both Belichick and Parcells had been promised decision-making powers with the Jets (according to Belichick's epilogue for this book, both he and Parcells were contractually promised the title of general manager), and Belichick wasn't about to take Parcells' claims of retirement seriously.

After his abrupt resignation, Belichick filed a grievance to void his Jets contract.

"Coach Belichick at the time did not have confidence that he would be put in complete control of the Jets in the manner he had been promised," said noted sports labor attorney Jeffrey Kessler, who represented Belichick. "We had good reason to believe that Parcells would be at a higher level. We felt [Parcells] would always be looking over Bill's shoulder."

Belichick lost the grievance, even though he proved to be correct in his assessment of Parcells' intentions. When the Jets later named Al Groh head coach, Parcells remained with the team as director of football operations. And three years later, despite repeated claims that he was done with the NFL, Parcells returned to the sidelines with the Dallas Cowboys.

After the failed grievance, Belichick took his case to the federal courts, which was the point when Parcells and Kraft finally got together and ended what Parcells called "the border war." Basically reversing the transaction between the teams just three years before, the Pats sent the Jets a package of draft picks (including a 2000 first-rounder) to bring Belichick to New England.

It was another time when history turned. Belichick signed a contract with Kraft that gave him complete autonomy over the football decisions, something that no Patriots coach had ever been granted in writing before. Two years later, the Pats were Super Bowl champions. Two years after that, they were Super Bowl champions again. The next year they won their third.

What caused the Krafts to change their organizational structure? Why, suddenly, were they willing to give the coach the power? Part of it had to do with the learning curve, as Carroll said. But most of it had to do with their confidence in Belichick.

"We knew Bill had the intellectual capacity to handle it," said Johnathan Kraft. "If you have the right people, the way we've operated with Bill is the way to do it. But, again, you have to have the right people."

Today, Robert and Johnathan are most definitely in the loop. They meet regularly with Belichick and personnel director Scott Pioli. The Krafts listen, then they step back and let Belichick and Pioli do their jobs. Since Belichick has taken over, he's traded franchise quarterback Drew Bledsoe, cut franchise safety Lawyer Milloy and traded for oft-troubled running back Corey Dillon. It's likely Kraft never would have allowed those moves in the early days of his ownership.

Pioli summed it up best: "They ask us questions—but they don't question us."

Tokens of the Krafts' journey and the Pats' success are everywhere. Johnathan Kraft has a pair of tickets from Chuck Sullivan's ill-fated Victory Tour framed in a picture behind his desk at Gillette Stadium. There is certainly more than one picture of Tom Brady, who Belichick and Pioli took a flyer on in the sixth round in 2000, hanging on the walls as well. And even though it's considered bad luck, Belichick just had to change the name of his boat in the spring of 2004. The boat had been christened the "Three Rings," representing his two titles as defensive coordinator of the Giants and his 2001 championship with the Pats. But after the Pats' Super Bowl XXXVIII win over Carolina, the boat naturally became the "Four Rings."

After 10 years at the helm, Robert Kraft is now one of the most powerful and respected owners in the NFL. The days of getting beat up by local politicians and hard-headed coaches are a thing of the past.

"Early on, I felt so fortunate to be in the position [of owner], but you're naïve in some ways, and you get caught up in certain things, and you get manipulated, you get beaten up a bit by the process," said Kraft. "This is a very tough business. And like anything, you learn. ...You go though the learning curve, and like any business, you figure out what the key things are, and you try to address them."

To be sure, the key things have been addressed. The result is a run of success that seemed well beyond the Patriots' reach. Prior to 1994, attendance was a constant problem and home games were frequently blacked out on local television. But under Kraft, the Pats have known nothing but sellouts (126 straight through the 2006 season) and every single game (including preseason) has been broadcast into the Boston market. The season-ticket base, which was often under 20,000, now stands at 61,000 with a paid waiting list of more than 50,000.

And, of course, there's the budding dynasty on the field.

People like Gino Cappelletti can only shake their heads at the current state of affairs. Cappelletti was there sitting on milk crates when Patriots players had to watch film projected onto bed sheets in a dank room beneath the stands at East Boston High School, and he was in the radio booths at the Superdome in New Orleans and Reliant Stadium in Houston when the Pats claimed their titles on the biggest stage in sports. Talk about extremes.

"I've seen some good years and as Bill Belichick would say, some not-so-good years," said Cappelletti. "And I've seen the best years—and that's what is happening right now. The Patriots are the absolute model of the league. Every team is aspiring to what the Patriots have got. This is it. The perfect owner. The perfect coach. They're all consistent. It's the best you could hope for."

With 12 straight wins to close out the 2003 regular season, and seven more to open 2004, the Patriots set an NFL record for consecutive victories (19). And to also open 2004—for the first time in their history—the Pats kicked off an entire NFL slate with a Thursday night win against Indianapolis.

"You think back 10 years, we just didn't want to be a doormat team," said Robert Kraft. "If you look back to the early '90s, I think the Patriots had the worst record in the league [between 1990-92]. We were fans and we were sitting there. And we were never proud of that. The postseason was always withdrawal. So it's pretty cool to be in that position [kicking off the NFL season], and doing it at our home field.

"When you think about it, before we [bought the team], we had no home playoff game victories. Only one home playoff game [in total]. Now we've been to three Super Bowls. We have a new stadium. We have all those fans on the waiting list and we have this thing positioned.

"It's something we can all take great pride in."

EPILOGUE

When I reflect on all that transpired on my way to becoming the head coach of the New England Patriots, I find myself more and more humbled by the accomplishments of our players and organization. It was a long and circuitous road, but one that has led to greater satisfaction than I could have imagined.

Several New England and Patriots-related events and circumstances have intertwined throughout my life and career. In one form or another, be it personal, educational, family or professional—close to 1,000 players, 100 coaches and 450 games—the one constant for me has always been New England. Wherever I've gone, wherever I've been, all roads seem to lead me back here.

In January 2000, Robert Kraft entered the picture and offered me the opportunity to coach the Patriots. Actually, I had known Robert for six years, dating back to our first meeting in January 1995, when I was head coach of the Browns. After the Browns eliminated the Patriots from the playoffs, Robert stopped by the Cleveland locker room to offer his congratulations to me—a classy move. In my whole career, I cannot recall any other owner, executive or coach doing this to my team.

Two years later I came to the Patriots as assistant head coach and developed a much closer relationship with Robert and found that our philosophies on business in football had many similarities. Our appearance in Super Bowl XXXI that season was a highlight in my coaching career to that point. Now, it pales in comparison to our recent championships. Robert has provided tremendous resources to the team, as well as great personal friendship through my years with the Patriots. It has been a very fruitful partnership.

I'm not a big believer in fate, so I doubt destiny was a determining factor in me winding up here. There's always more logic to it than that. But as I reflect on my career, I'm amazed how closely connected I was to the Patriots, years and decades before I even realized it.

For example, my first year in the league was with the Baltimore Colts in 1975. We started off the season very badly, the low point being a 21-10 loss to the Patriots in October that dropped our record to 1-4. Our fans were upset, the press was all over us and the consensus was this was a lost season. From then on, however, we proceeded to win our last nine games of the year (including a 34-21 win over New England to close out the regular season) and win the division. I often think back on that great lesson learned early in my career—not judging a season based on the first month, staying the course and focusing on getting better every week.

Another interesting twist involving the Patriots began in 1976. Actually, it goes back to 1975. One of my training camp assignments with the Colts was to break down a playoff game from the previous season between the Rams and Redskins. In this game, the Rams employed a two tight end set, which was very unusual in those days. This personnel group was a new wrinkle that gave Washington's defense a lot of problems and contributed greatly to the Rams winning the game. So I studied the game thoroughly.

The next year, when I was coaching the tight ends in Detroit, we were getting ready to play the 3-1 Patriots, who were loaded that year and coming off consecutive huge wins over Miami, Pittsburgh, and Oakland. This was really one of the best teams in Patriots history. After a lot of discussion and some major changes on our coaching staff, we decided to use some of the same multiple tight end concepts that the Rams used in their playoff win. Again, using two tight ends was still pretty new at the time, but we were 1-3, our head coach had resigned, and we were willing to try something for a spark.

Our two tight end set featured Charlie Sanders and our second-round draft choice from 1976, David Hill. Essentially, offenses in those days were set up with three receivers on one side and two on the other—or "strong side/weak side." (this is the same basic principle you'd see when studying basketball's 5 on 5) But the balanced two tight end set essentially created two strong sides at the snap of the ball. In succeeding years, defenses adjusted to this set, which has become common in the NFL. But in 1976, it was a major problem for the defense.

Well, we won the game we had no business winning, 30-10, and from that point on, Chuck Fairbanks, the Patriots head coach, called a two tight end offense "Detroit" based on that game.

Coach Fairbanks's term stood the test of time and here is why. Ron Erhardt was Fairbanks's offensive coordinator, so ever since that game against us, the Fairbanks-Erhardt-Parcells-Weis-Belichick group called two tight ends "Detroit." And that remains with us to this day. Think about it. I'm a 24-year-old in Detroit who, in an incredibly roundabout way, contributes to a term used 30 years later in another organization...one that I happen to be coaching. There are hundreds of little anecdotes like this floating around the league. I love this one.

There are more New England connections. More than any other team, I just seemed to have established and maintained more relationships with coaches from the Patriots staff than other teams. Think about some of the coaches who coached here in the 70s: Red Miller (who was my boss in Denver in 1978), Ray Perkins (who hired me at the Giants in 1979), Bill Parcells, Ron Erhardt, Ernie Adams (a classmate of mine from Andover who worked in the same capacity with New England in '75 as I did at Baltimore) and Rollie Dotch. I ended up working with all of them at other teams. It's just interesting for me to look back on it. It's probably mostly just luck of the draw but there's still an undeniable connection between the Patriots and me that runs very deep.

That brings me to one of my deepest rooted passions—my fondness for this area of the country. To be here, now, in this position, is more good fortune than I could ever dream of. From my office, it takes an hour and a half to get to Nantucket, a summer retreat of mine for over 30 years. I've spent more hours on the former Woods Hole ferry (now Hyannis) than I'll admit, not to mention the commuter airlines. I graduated from Phillips Academy after a postgraduate year and went on to four years at Wesleyan University in Connecticut. I still remember driving up to Boston College football, Celtics-Knicks, Patriots-Jets and Bruins-Rangers games in the 70s.

Some other events stand out in my mind, too.

One of my most vivid New England memories was in 1973, when I was on my way from Annapolis to Nantucket. I stopped in Plymouth Harbor to tour Mayflower II, the replica of the boat carrying 102 passengers trip to the new world. Seeing that incredibly small boat and thinking about how it crossed the Atlantic in 1620 gives me great appreciation for what our forefathers did when they settled this country.

Another story dates to the spring of 1984, when I planned on spending a quiet Easter weekend on Nantucket. Guess what? Instead of a quiet Easter—a nor'easter blew in and knocked down two of the island's sturdiest landmarks. One was a huge, full, beautiful, 80-foot oak tree in our neighbors' yard. The other was the Great Point Lighthouse, which crumbled into the sea after being pummeled by waves and wind.

Now, 20 years later, through the great strength that characterizes our New England land and seascape, both monuments still remain. The oak, lying on its side, still lives with new trunks literally growing out of the original root system. And Great Point was rebuilt as rocks were ferried to the northernmost point on Nantucket for construction in the dunes of sand.

Never was the strength of character that defines New Englanders more evident than with our 2001 and 2003 players who, through their unselfish commitment to teamwork and ability to focus, prepare, and execute under pressure, made us all champions.

I love New England, its seasons, tradition and people and I feel privileged, thankful and proud to be part of its colorful history as one person among a team of championship players and an organization of terrific people.

—Bill Belichick
Nantucket, Massachusetts
July, 2006